Bonne Journée
MADAME

Published under licence by Brown Dog Books and
The Self-Publishing Partnership Ltd, 10b Greenway Farm, Bath Rd,
Wick, nr. Bath BS30 5RL

www.selfpublishingpartnership.co.uk

ISBN printed book: 978-1-83952-496-7
ISBN e-book: 978-1-83952-497-4

Cover design by Kevin Rylands
Internal design by Andrew Easton

Printed and bound in the UK

This book is printed on FSC certified paper

Bonne Journée Madame

JILL McCORD

BROWN
DOG
BOOKS

"Bonne Journée Madame"

We were on the autobahn driving back through France. I was sitting in the back seat of the car with my daughter feeling utterly desolate and not wanting to return home. I was distracted by watching lots of camper vans passing us by. An idea of escape started to form in my mind. I turned to my daughter and said in a low voice, "Let's buy a camper van and travel around France." She replied instantly, momentarily excited, "Yes, let's do it Mum!"

That was the beginning of our adventure.

In 2002 when I was aged 52, my husband, who was fifteen years older than me, died suddenly from an aortic aneurism.

The shock, pain and grief were incalculable. I was barely functioning. My daughter aged twenty-two had not long graduated from Camberwell College of Arts in London.

My husband and I had been due to go for a long weekend to Brittany with friends who owned a house there. They had very kindly suggested that I should still go with them and that my daughter Phillippa could accompany me. It was very hard to go alone without my husband, but I needed to get away and it was a distraction. I felt with my daughter for support I could face going, so we took up our friends' invitation and travelled with them in their car.

The thought of "escaping" to France sustained me for the next nine months. Not long before my husband died, I had left my job as a school secretary which I had done for over fourteen years. I wanted a change and was ready to embark on a different career. In the meantime, I had been working as a temporary secretary, taking on different contracts. After my husband died, it was all I could do initially to get from day to day, hour to hour. There was so much to do practically, sorting out funeral arrangements and all the paperwork, running the house. Some days it was as much as I could do to just put the kettle on. My mind and body were in turmoil, and I was permanently in a state of exhaustion.

As time went on, I had to return to the workplace not only for my own sanity but I needed to for financial reasons. I started applying for part-time jobs. It was hard filling out application forms and writing letters of application. This was in the days before everything went online.

I was successful in being offered a temporary six-month contract as a medical secretary. I was grateful to be in an office on my own and not having to interact with the other office staff. I don't think they were aware of my circumstances apart from the practice manager who had offered me the job. I sat at the keyboard with my audio earphones plugged into my ears and a medical dictionary by my side, typing up the doctor's notes. I hated it, but it was a distraction for my mind as I had to concentrate on something other than my grief.

After four hours I could escape and drive home and go for a long walk in the fresh air with my dog, Milo. It was good therapy for my well-being and helped focus my mind. It also gave me time to plan my trip to France. It all seemed an impossible dream but the thought of being able to go sustained me.

One day, I received a letter from my late husband's employers. As his widow, I was entitled to a monthly pension and in my circumstance a discretionary lump sum. Some weeks letter, a cheque arrived in the post for the sum of £10,000. This was my camper van money and God's provision. I was meant to go, I was sure.

I hadn't the first clue about camper vans but some very dear friends of ours who lived in our village had been camper van devotees for years. They gave me advice as to what to look for. The hunt was on. After a few fruitless expeditions, I contacted a local firm who told me one had just come on to the forecourt. It had not even been valeted. I contacted my friend who willingly accompanied me and my daughter to inspect the camper van. The price being asked for the van was £10,000 !! How amazing was that? Another confirmation to me that my trip to France would go ahead. We went out on a test drive with Phillippa doing the driving. My knowledgeable friend felt the camper was a good buy, and so I went ahead and bought it. The said camper van was a Fiat Swift Royale. We later named him "Escargot" which of course is French for snail, as he would become our home on our backs for the next few months.

Escargot was duly valeted and serviced. The next problem was where to store him until we were able to leave for France.

A farmer who lived at the top of my lane in the village where I lived kindly offered to let me park Escargot on his small campsite, free of charge.

At the time I had a beautiful black and white border collie called Milo. He was two years old, full of vitality and highly intelligent. We loved him dearly and there was no way we would leave him behind. He had to come to France too.

The rules for pets travelling abroad in 2002 included having a pet passport and an up-to- date rabies inoculation.

From the outset, I had wanted to be out of the country before the first anniversary of my husband's death on the 9th May and what would have been our wedding anniversary later that month.

I made an appointment with the vet and took Milo. The rabies inoculation would need to be done in two doses and the vet informed me I would not be able to return to England with Milo before three and a half months. That's fine, I thought. We will go for three and a half months then.

The proposed trip of course had to be financed. I started looking into the possibility of letting my two-bedroom bungalow. This proved more difficult than I had envisaged. All the letting agents I contacted were not interested in a short-term tenancy agreement for a furnished property. To let as a holiday home was not possible either as someone needed to be on hand for changeovers and cleaning. I was beginning to give up hope until a friend suggested I contact a firm called "Paul Property" in Topsham, a nearby town. I telephoned Paul who didn't seem to feel there was any problem; he was sure he could find tenants for me. I arranged for Paul to come and view my home. Over coffee, I told him of my circumstances and my plan to go to France. He asked me what I did for a living, and I told him I had a temporary contract at a doctors' surgery, but I wasn't happy in my job situation. We got on to estate agency. I shared with him how some years ago I had worked for various estate agents and how much I had enjoyed the work and found it very interesting. "Well," Paul replied, "as it happens I am looking for someone to help out in my office." My ears pricked up. "But I am planning to be in France for three and a half months," I responded. "How will that work...?" "Not a problem," said Paul. "The job will still be there when you return."

I gave in my notice at the doctors' surgery. It was such a relief to go. I commenced working at Paul Property which I enjoyed very much. Topsham is a friendly community, and I worked with a lovely lady who was very supportive towards me. One day I was asked to show a couple of chaps around a property in the town. They had come from Wales to be "troubleshooters" at a large insurance company nearby. The property which I showed them around wasn't suitable for their requirements. Walking back to the office, they explained they were on a short-term contract and needed somewhere to live during the week but would travel home at weekends. I told them that I happened know of a very nice property which was located just over two miles away from the insurance company where they would be working. They immediately expressed an interest and wanted to know all about it. I told them that it was a lovely bungalow, and I knew this because it was my own home.

We arranged a suitable day and time for me to meet them at my address. When they had viewed my bungalow, I explained to the chaps my reasons why I was going to let my home: the fact that my husband had died and of my planned trip to France. They were very sympathetic and at the same time rather in admiration of what I intended to do. It was a done deal, and the necessary contract was drawn up through Paul Property.

Paul recommended that before I vacated my home, I should store away any personal effects such as photographs. I had quite a few houseplants and these I distributed amongst willing friends and neighbours before our departure.

One day when I was at work, a guy I knew who used to attend my local church came into the office. Wynn and his French wife Marie had a house in Topsham but had been living in France. We greeted each other warmly. Wynn had no idea that my husband had died and was very shocked and saddened to hear the news. When I told him about my proposed trip to France, Wynn said that we must come and visit and stay with them. Wynn and Marie lived near the French/Swiss border in a town called Divonne les Bains. He wrote down his address and contact details. I promised him that once we were in France, we would go and visit them. This was another affirmation in my mind that I was meant to go.

As my daughter and I had never been away in the camper van, we were strongly advised that we should have a trial run before we left the country. The date set for our departure was the 2nd of May. We decided to go away over the long Easter break in April for three nights. I booked us in at a small campsite at Tedburn St. Mary which was not many miles away. We really were novices and had not realised all that was entailed in owning a camper van. We had to work out how to use the gas cooker, how to fill up the water tank and how to empty the toilet. I remember that we were really cold at night as it was only early April.

Still, we survived and managed to drive there and back.

The day for our departure was drawing ever closer. So many people said to me that they thought I was very brave to be heading off to France in a camper van for that length of time. I didn't feel brave at all. I was running away. I could not have entertained the trip if my daughter Phillippa had not been able to come with me.

We were given lots of helpful advice as to what to take with us in the van. A friend lent us a small fold-up camping table to use for eating outside, and I invested in two small fold-up camping chairs. We were limited to how much we could pack into Escargot. We packed what clothes we deemed suitable for every weather condition but kept them to a minimum. We took non-perishable food and the necessary plates, cutlery and cooking utensils. I limited saucepans to two. Everyone said that we would be able to buy anything else we needed from a *supermarché* in France because everything would be much cheaper. In fact, this proved to be not necessarily the case. We took as many books as we could to read, and I had bought travel journals to keep a blog of our travels. Milo, of course, had to

Campsite at Chamonix

Annecy campsite, Milo being brushed

'Escargot' awaiting new tyre (Pneu)

Night time trip to shower block - spooky

What a lovely sight, the clanging of the bells get louder and louder

Milo hears cat mewing inside shut-up house

"Nightmare" drive around Gorges du Verdon

be provided for, and I bought a large bag of dried food plus Bonio dog biscuits etc. and his food and water bowls and his dog blanket. I triple checked that I had packed all the necessary paperwork in a folder, passports, Insurance documents and Milo's pet travel scheme certificate showing proof of vaccine for rabies. Last but not least, I had the 2003 "Alan Rogers' book of quality campsites in France" which would prove invaluable initially.

We were also given tips by friends of their favourite places to visit in France. I had a large map of the country and had ringed places of interest. We had decided to travel the Route Napoleon. The guidebooks termed it: "one of the best drives through France – Route Napoleon is a 200-mile stretch of modern road winding through the spectacular mountains of Provence. The road follows the route taken by Napoleon in his 1815 escape from Elba to Grenoble." It all sounded very exciting, and we wanted to visit all those romantic places in the South of France and the Côte d'Azur.

We were taking two bicycles with us (which later proved to be a godsend). Our friend D came over on the morning we left and secured the bikes on the rack at the back of the van. I spent the last hour in my bungalow on my hands and knees, washing the kitchen floor. We had cleaned the rest of the bungalow thoroughly beforehand in readiness for our tenants.

Our adventure has begun. A small group of friends and neighbours has gathered outside to wave us off and take photographs. We had arranged to cross from Dover to Calais. During the planning of the trip, I plumped for this crossing as it was the shortest route. I am worried about having to leave Milo shut up in the van on his own.

Once we are on board the ferry, we have to leave Escargot and go up on deck and cannot return to the van until we embark.

Our drive to Dover takes over six hours. We are quite exhausted by the time we arrive, what with all the emotional farewells beforehand and the long drive. We camp up on the side of the dock and spend the night ready for the 7 am crossing to Calais. I am petrified that we will oversleep and miss the crossing. There is no fear of that as there is so much activity going on early that morning; we really needn't have bothered to set the alarm. When Phillippa finally drives the van up the gangway onto the ferry, she says excitedly, "Mum do you realise that we are off to France for three and a half months?" Indeed we were. I still can't believe it. It doesn't help lessen my high level of anxiety. I am permanently exhausted. Only those who have experienced bereavement will understand how grief affects every fibre of one's being and my mind seems to be constantly in turmoil. Only sleep brings brief respite.

The crossing passes very quickly, and Milo survives being left alone in the camper van. We duly arrive at Calais and take the A26 road, Calais to Reims. Before our departure, I had pre-booked a campsite for our first night at a place called Le Vivier aux Carpes, which as its name implies, was situated beside carp ponds. I quickly get used to driving on the right- hand side of the road and drive the majority of the way towards Arras and Soissons to Seraucourt-le-Grand. It is exciting that all the other camper van drivers wave to us as they pass, and of course we wave back. I am relatively confident to drive on the autobahn but once we get on to the minor roads, Phillippa does all the driving (she became quite an expert and drove Escargot as if it were a mini car). I am content to attempt to do the navigating, which on occasions caused some arguments – but more of that later.

When we arrive at the campsite, we find it to be very quiet; not many people are camping this early on in the season. We enjoy walking Milo around the carp ponds. Milo was our priority: he needed a lot of exercise, especially after he had been cooped up in the van whilst we were travelling. I fill up the water container which became a daily chore, as well as emptying the toilet. We only used the toilet at night to go for a wee, otherwise we used the campsite toilets. Nonetheless, it had to be emptied every day. That first evening in France, we walk into the village to have a meal in a local café – steak and *frites*, a glacé and beer to drink. We had arrived in France and we had the whole trip still ahead of us; how exciting was that! In bed by 10 pm., shattered.

Phillippa sleeps above the driver's seat where there was a cabin bed. She doesn't bother with the ladder but legs it up and draws the curtains across. This gives her some privacy and space. I sleep on the sofa seat by the little dining table. The seats could be pulled out to form a bed, but I am perfectly comfortable lying on the single seat with a pillow and duvet. I am always so tired, so sleep easily. Milo sleeps on his rug under the table next to me. In the morning, I only have to roll up the duvet and pillow. It saves a lot of time and hassle.

The following day, we drive to the local *intermarché*. We drive past flat, open fields of rape lined with poplar trees. We do a big food shop at the *intermarché*, and I buy a washing up bowl and bucket which I had forgotten to bring with us from home. I am struck again on entering the *intermarché*, which I have experienced before and since, of that peculiar smell French supermarkets seem to have: a mixture of slightly soar used dishcloths and raw meat.

We head back to the site and make a cup of tea. Phillippa gives Milo a good brush which he loves. We sit down to work out our expenses and how much we have spent so far. I am somewhat taken aback at how much we have spent already in just two days. I am determined to keep a tighter budget, otherwise we will run out of money. These were the days before I had internet banking.

We walk Milo around the carp ponds again and watch men sitting fishing. We return to Escargot and have a simple supper of jambon, rice and salad, followed by fruit, Port Salut and bread, washed down with a glass of red wine.

The next morning, we give Milo a quick walk around the lake and then get ready for the off. We finally leave at 12.00 noon. We are realising what has to be done; it is always my job to empty the toilet in the sluice and wash it out, the water tank needs to be filled, and everything secured. We do speed up with the whole procedure as time goes on, but at this stage we are very much on a learning curve.

I navigate as Phillippa drives. She is much happier to be the driver; I don't think she trusts me behind the wheel. We take the D1 towards Soissons, trying to avoid autoroutes. We pass through Chauny, a pleasant, small town. Everywhere looks so clean and tidy, a bit like a "Lego" town. The countryside is pretty but still very flat. We pass through typical French villages with lots of pantiles. They all seem deserted with not even a dog wandering around. I have often wondered before and since why French villages always seem so forsaken.

Where does everyone go?! We stop off at a picnic site on the Gunyon de l'Oise and l'Aisne canal and sit beside the canal and watch barges go by while Milo swims. There are big Charolais cattle in the fields opposite, and we hear the cuckoo for the first time.

We drive on towards Chateau Thierry and Montmirail. It's now very hot. We carry on along the D373 heading for Suzanne and then on to the N4. Navigating and driving are going well until on reaching Vitry-le-François, we hear a funny whooshing noise. We pull over and realise we have a puncture. Slight panic. Phillippa rings roadside recovery. Her GCSE French is far better than my virtually non-existent vocabulary. Eventually, a very sweet French mechanic arrives and changes the tyre. We soon learn the French word for tyre is "*pneu.*" We follow him to the nearby garage where he puts in air. After many "*merci beaucoup*" we drive on towards Saint-Dizier. It is now starting to get dusky. We finally arrive at the campsite on Lac Der-Chantecoq. Now dark. Give Milo a quick swim and walk on beach, supper and fall into bed.

We wake to an almost deserted campsite. It is still very early in the season. It is a beautiful, sunny morning, and I head for the shower block and watch lots of house martins flying in and out to their nests. Later, we walk around part of the lake, which we discover is the largest man-made lake in Europe. We keep to the cycle track and Milo has lots of swims. We need to keep him cool in the heat. Arriving back at the site, we sit outside a little cafe overlooking the lake. We order two beers. Freedo, our friendly barman, is obviously taken with Phillippa and we score two free beers!!

We drive to the nearby small village and buy a few provisions in the local shop. There is no fresh milk though, only UHT which we can't abide. We soon learn to shop in *supermarchés* which stock fresh milk in cartons. After a simple supper of salad and bread and cheese, we study the map and the "Rough Guide" which I had brought with us.

I am still feeling anxious about how long it will take us to get down to the South and about our finances. It is only our sixth day. I know primarily it is because I am finding it hard to relax. I am still exhausted from the grief and trauma of the last year.

This morning we make an earlier start. I settle the bill with the campsite owner, who is very friendly and speaks good English. I buy some croissants from him for breakfast. We leave at 9.30 am and head for Troyes, capital town of the Champagne/Ardennes area. Much cooler and cloudier today. We find Troyes to have many medieval, timbered houses. We decide to leave Milo in the van and have a mooch around the town. It has a large Gothic cathedral. Eventually, we find a covered market where we buy some fruit, olives and anchovies and sun-dried tomatoes. We take them back to the van for lunch. I am writing down everything we spend in a notebook. We take the N19 towards Chaumont. We stop at a small town called Bessancourt and walk Milo around a park, once the grounds of a large chateau, now all boarded up with crumbling walls. I would love to have known who had once lived there and learnt about its fascinating history.

We carry on to Langres. The countryside here is much more undulating, and it is good to feel the warmth of the sun. We pass many fields of dazzling yellow rape. Unfortunately, we discover that the campsite at Langres does not open until June! We retrace our steps to the small hamlet of Humes where we find a dear little campsite by a river. This is where my OS map comes into its own, as it depicts campsites with the symbol of a black tent (remember this was in the days before satnav). We find a pitch, whereupon the farmer's wife appears with her baby in her arms, to collect our money. She makes a great fuss of Milo, as do an English couple who have just arrived from Calais on their way to Italy. (How, I wonder, did they manage to get from Calais to here in just over six hours?). Milo is loving all the attention and getting lots of stick throwing by the English guy.

We have been feeling cut off from friends and family at home. Phillippa has brought her laptop with her, but for some reason we cannot access our emails. It looks as if we will have to wait until we arrive at Wynn and Marie's house and use their internet. It is all very frustrating.

It is lovely to wake up on our dear little site and watch house martins swooping and dipping in the river whilst we eat our breakfast and enjoy an early cup of tea. We are not so slow at packing up today. I feel we are getting more to grips with what has to be done. From the campsite, we drive into Langres which is a beautiful old walled town, set high above the River Marne. Having parked Escargot, we walk Milo around the ramparts of the old walls with their spectacular views. The town is full of beautiful, shuttered houses with pots of red geraniums lining the window sills. This makes me feel that we have truly arrived in France and I am beginning to feel much more relaxed. We pass a boulangerie and I cannot resist going in for a tarte aux fraises because everything looks so delicious. Surely I can allow myself the odd treat? The smiling lady behind the counter calls, "*Bonne journée madame*" as I leave the shop. "*Merci beaucoup*," I reply. Yes, I do feel that I am having a good day; my spirits have lifted.

Our next destination is Auxonne. We stop off at an *intermarché* for food and petrol. I still feel anxious that we are spending too much money but don't feel that we are being extravagant. I have located a campsite is one not in the "Alan Rogers" book. It is alongside a canal and for the first time, we put our garden chairs outside and sit and enjoy a glass of rosé wine. The campsite is very quiet which means Milo can roam freely. I give Escargot a good spring clean as we have been treading in lots of mown grass.

We stay one night on this site and then decide we will visit Auxonne where we park Escargot in a side street and taking Milo with us, we have a wonder around the town which seems almost deserted. We decide it must be a Bank Holiday or Saints Day (of which there seem to be many in France) as most of the shops are closed. There is a large army barracks here, where I read that apparently Bonaparte was once a cadet. We seem to be getting into a smooth rhythm now, with Phillippa doing the driving and me navigating; however, we are still on fairly major roads. We take the D24 and head for Beaune, a town that we know, having stayed there once on a family holiday when en route for Annecy. I wonder how I will feel going back to a place where I had been with my late husband.

The countryside we drive through is pretty and rural; we admire the different coloured irises growing in gardens. The campsite is on the edge of Beaune and is very clean and well equipped. Each plot has a beech hedge around it with its own washing line. Once ensconced, we walk with Milo into Beaune. We remember it well. I really like the town; it's so attractive with its many squares and pavement cafes. The joy of our campsite is that because it's so close to the town, we can walk to and from Beaune without having to move Escargot. Having explored, we head back to the campsite and take advantage of the washing line by doing a load of washing in the site washing machine. We learn as time goes on that many of the campsite washing machines are heavy duty and wreck our clothes. We are careful therefore to wash delicates by hand. Whilst waiting for the washing to complete its cycle, I get chatting to a nice Dutch lady, who of course speaks perfect English. How come the Dutch speak so many languages? I guess because no one else speaks Dutch BUT the Dutch! We meet many Dutch people on our travels, and they are always so friendly and pleasant to talk to.

It is the morning of the 9th May which is the first anniversary of my husband's death. We are in a reflective mood this morning and take our time, being very aware of the significance of today's date. We can hardly believe that somehow we have managed to get through a whole year of grief and that already we have now been a week in France. If anyone had told me on that dreadful day that a year hence I would find myself in a camper van, travelling around France with Phillippa, I would have struggled to believe them. Before we left home, friends had given me cards which I had brought with us to be opened on this anniversary date. We are very moved by the words which they contain and are comforted by them. We do the usual chores and I fill up the water tank. It's surprising how long all these tasks take, and of course Milo has to have a walk before we can leave.

We are heading for Tornus and we drive through our first vineyards and past fields of barley rolling like the sea, rippling in the breeze. We are now in the Burgundy region where some of the best French wines are produced. We manage to park Escargot by the river Saone with barges moored alongside. We walk with Milo through the town and discover the lovely old Abbey of St. Philibert dating back to 900 AD. We go inside. It is very beautiful, and we feel that this is where we are meant to be today. It is so peaceful and reverent. We light a candle in memory of my husband, and we sit quietly together and reflect. Afterwards, we return to Escargot not speaking a word to one another, but in silence, each with our own thoughts.

Once inside the van, I make a much-needed cup of tea. We read the many text messages we have received and talk to family and friends on our mobile phones who are remembering us especially today.

Eventually we leave and drive to Macon as dusk falls. We manage to find a site on the edge of Macon which is large and well equipped with lots of hedges. The next day I am anxious to head off and get away from the busy town. I am eager to meet up with Wynn and Marie. It has been a week since we have had any real conversation other than that between ourselves. We are getting into some sort of routine now. We use the campsite facilities during the day but use the camper van toilet at night. It is my job to empty the contents of the toilet into the sluice each morning and wash it out.

We drive away from bustling Macon, stopping by the Saone river, and give Milo a good walk along the banks. I make coffee and we have a picnic lunch in Escargot, then continue on the N79 towards Bourgeois en Brussels and Ceyzeriat to Nantua. It is much more mountainous country now and the roads twist and turn uphill. I am very thankful once again that Phillippa is doing the driving. She has become very competent and drives Escargot with ease. There is very much the Swiss influence here as we are nearing the Swiss border. The scenery is quite spectacular: pine forests, lakes, mountains and gorges, chalet houses and Swiss-type churches with pointed spires. We are nearing Divonne le Bain and so I ring Wynn to tell him we are on our way. He arranges to drive to Divonne to meet us, bringing one of his small sons with him. It is wonderful to greet Wynn who gives us a hug and a kiss on both our cheeks. We follow his car as he drives back to his and Marie's lovely home. On arrival we are met with a warm welcome from Marie and their other son. We are invited to sit outside on their terrace where we are given a much appreciated cup of tea. It is just so lovely to be with them and to be able to talk about so much. Later on, I offer to take the two little boys for a walk with Milo, who they think is absolutely wonderful. We walk through lush green meadows into some nearby woods. The landscape feels very Swiss. The boys are eager to show Phillippa and me their pet rabbit which they keep in a hutch. Milo spends the rest of the afternoon sitting in front of the hutch, his eyes fixed intently on the lapin, as if watching television. It is very amusing, but I am not sure if the poor lapin finds it so.

In the evening we sit around the table and hold hands for grace. Marie and Wynn have prepared us a delicious meal. It is so uplifting to be in a family home again. Marie chatters on in French and tries to teach us some phrases. After the boys have gone to bed, we clear away and sit and chat for ages. Feeling tired, we say our good nights. I have a wonderful bath. It feels fabulous to have the space and luxury of a bathroom and house. It makes a pleasant interlude after the camper van and we have only been in it a week! We retire for the night to Escargot which we have parked on their drive. Wynn and Marie are lovely and so welcoming.

I take Milo for a walk at 8 am. The air feels so fresh, and the mountains look beautiful in the sunshine. We have our breakfast with the family and then as it is *Dimanche*, we leave for church at 9.30 am. Wynn takes us all in his large Espace. We are attending the "Crossroads Church" in Ferney-Voltaire. It is an English-speaking Interdenominational Church. After the service we go into the church lounge where there is a cake sale. Wynn introduces us to various people. Suddenly, I hear loud exclamations and squealing. Who should be embracing Phillippa but Elaine, one of her friends from London. We can't believe our eyes. Elaine was on holiday staying with friends in Geneva. She had no idea we would be in the area. What a small world and how amazing. We arrange to meet up with Elaine in Geneva the following day.

We spend the rest of Sunday with Wynn and Marie at their home. That night there is a terrific thunderstorm with hailstones which clatter on Escargot's roof, keeping us awake, which is quite spectacular. By morning the storm has blown over, and we wake to blue skies and sunshine. Our hosts had left early to go to Lausanne on business. We had said our farewells and profuse thank yous the night before.

It is a luxury to have their house to ourselves. We breakfast and shower – oh the joy of a hairdryer! Phillippa does a load of washing in the washing machine and hangs it out to dry. Milo continues to stand and stare at the rabbit cage. He is so funny to watch. I think he would stand there all day – mesmerised. On Wynn's recommendation, we drive into nearby Gex to try and get a spare tyre for Escargot. Would you believe the garage is closed? We try another garage in Divonne, but they are out of stock of that particular *pneu*! All very frustrating. We carry on towards Geneva and cross the Swiss border. We are in Switzerland. How exciting. We park high above Lac Leman and walk down steps to the lake, taking the path beside it into Geneva itself, going past the famous fountain shooting its water high into the sky. We rendezvous with Elaine and walk to the old part of Geneva, impressed by the expensive shops and elegantly attired ladies. We idle away a pleasant hour or so sitting at an outside café, enjoying a bottle of beer. Having finally said our farewells to Elaine, we walk back the way we came, and Milo has his daily swim. I had booked a campsite found in the "Alan Rogers" guide. It is in a beautiful situation right on Lake Leman, expensive but worth it for the stunning situation and the view. The lake is full of ducks and swans.

Unfortunately, we are plagued by mosquitoes and get bitten which rather detracts from the idyllic location. It is as well we are only staying one night as the campsite tariffs are high. It is definitely a case of location, location.

We wake to clouds; Lac Leman is really quite choppy. We drive around Leman to Thonan and Evian. Despite the clouds, the view is still awesome as we look across the lake to the mountains. We make a stop at Evian but everywhere is shut because it is lunch time. It is really raining now, so we decide to drive through Montraux and make for Martigny. It is not much fun driving in heavy rain with the wipers going. I am thankful to be going back into France as Switzerland is so expensive. The N506 takes us over a mountain pass to Chamonix. It's an absolutely spectacular drive around hairpin bends and once again I am very relieved that Phillippa is doing the driving. The rain has gone, and we descend into Chamonix with mountains above us and valleys below. Our campsite, Les Rosières, according to Alan Rogers "is one of the most spectacular settings imaginable for a campsite with the scenic grandeur of the Alps towering above and within a 15-minute walk of Chamonix by way of a river."

We are not disappointed: the site lives up to the description. Poor Milo has not been walked all day apart from our stop at Evian. We walk him along a footpath by a fast-flowing stream into the almost empty ski resort with chair lifts suspended above the mountains. I study the map of the ski runs. I haven't skied for over twenty years. Once safely back in Escargot we have our supper. It is really cold now. We fill our hot water bottles and batten down the hatches for the night... all snug. At long last we are able to access our emails. We are delighted to find that we have eighteen messages. We are just like two children on Christmas Eve it is so exciting. It is so good to be in contact with people again and catch up on their news. We spend time replying to some of them.

I don't have a particularly good night's sleep as I'm really cold and at one point I have to put my fleecy top on. I rise at 7 am and step outside to a crisp, sunny morning and am met with an awesome sight of snow-capped mountains with pine trees all around. Wow! It really is stunning. There are very few other campers on the site as it is early season – only a few intrepid walkers and a guy next to us in a camper van. He seemed rather a sad figure sitting outside his van all alone eating his boiled eggs. I did say "good morning" but got the impression he did not wish to engage in conversation. He was probably perfectly happy and maybe couldn't speak English? I take Milo and walk back along the footpath into Chamonix. It is still cold but with beautiful sunshine. I decide it is better to be here out of season before the crowds arrive. Once back at the van, I brew up some coffee and sit with Phillippa as we pour over the map and discuss our next route. We will be taking the D909 to Annecy. We know what a beautiful town Annecy is as we had stayed there some years ago on holiday with my husband and friends when Phillippa was aged nine.

Our route to Annecy takes us through the Grande Alps, along twisty, windy roads with huge drops down into the valleys below and soaring mountains above. Quite hairy in places. The scenery really is spectacular and has a decidedly Swiss influence. We pass many "music box" type chalet houses and see creamy coloured cows with huge bells around their necks grazing in the meadows. At one point we are forced to stop on a road to allow a herd of cows pass by with their clanging bells suspended from their necks, being driven along by the farmer for milking. Such a charming sight. It really has been a beautiful journey and well worth the twists and turns. Phillippa has again excelled herself with her driving expertise and so far I have managed with the navigating. I use the Alan Rogers book once again and have found a campsite on the edge of Annecy which overlooks the lake. It is still only early May and we have no need to worry about campsites being full.

We make a decision to spend a few days here in Annecy. It will be good to relax rather than constantly moving on and driving. Also campsites can be very transient, and we hope that by staying put for a while, we may get to know other people. We put the camping chairs up that morning and sit outside Escargot to soak up the sun. Later we walk into Annecy.

Phillippa has taken her rollerblades and she blades around the lake on the designated path. I stroll around with Milo. Annecy is beautiful; there are swans and ducks on the lake, people are boating, the snow glistens on the snow-capped mountains. Everyone is out promenading, mothers with babies in prams, people blading – they go in for it in a big way over here, all age groups and sexes. Old people sitting on seats and chatting, lovers sunbathing on the grass. Although surrounded by people, I still feel incredibly alone. I am pleased Phillippa is having fun; she needs to have time on her own and we need space from one another.

When we return to Escargot, we discover that another British camper van has arrived on site. We start chatting to the couple who it belongs to and they tell us that they are on their way home from Provence. Later, Phillippa goes to the washroom to wash up the dishes after supper and starts talking to a lovely Scottish lady. When Phillippa shares with her our circumstances and the reason we are travelling, the lady thinks it is a wonderful trip we are undertaking and is very impressed. She and her husband are travelling in France for a month.

We wake up to another gorgeous morning and actually have breakfast sitting outside on our fold-up chairs. I do a machine load of washing and hang it out to dry on the washing line we have rigged up. I discover that Milo has picked up a lot of ticks from somewhere. Yuk! I spend a pleasant half an hour removing the ticks. Whilst pegging out the washing, I meet an English guy called Rob who is really into paragliding. He and his mate are travelling around in a converted red van. He comes from Reading and has given up his job and intends travelling the world. I am not sure how he is financing the trip. He thinks what Phillippa and I are doing is great. I had to explain to Rob about how my husband had died which is never an easy thing to do. He seems a nice chap. I also have a long chat with an English couple in a camper van who it turns out are from Manchester. Their van seems immaculate compared to ours; it looks so pristine. The couple are very friendly and give me lots of information about other campsites to visit once we get nearer to Provence. It is a great boost to be meeting more people and able to talk to others now that we are settled here for a few days.

After lunch, I walk with Phillippa and Milo into Annecy with the intention of finding a bank. I am hoping to be able to establish the state of my bank balance and get a statement printed. I am told by the cashier in the bank that this will not be possible and advised to go on the internet. However, at this time I do not have internet banking set up. Even though I am writing down everything we spend, it is difficult to keep tabs of what is going in and out of my current account.

Phillippa has gone off around the shops as she has decided she needs some sandals. I sit with Milo by the canal and write postcards. When we first came to Annecy, it was at the height of summer, and all the bridges were thick with baskets of red geraniums. The bridges seem quite bare now in May. When we return to Escargot, we find that two more camper vans and two caravans have arrived and have parked around us. The occupants are British, except for one German couple. We have lost our quiet little corner. They all seem to be retired couples which I do find hard because it just brings home to me my situation and how I miss my husband so.

After supper, Phillippa takes Milo and goes off blading again around the lake. I am content to sit outside and do some writing.

The following morning we are surprised to be woken by heavy rain which is such a contrast to the last few days. I don't feel terribly inspired to get moving and so lie on my bed and read. Phillippa gives Milo a quick trip outside to do his "jobbies" and then spends time writing some emails. The rain eventually eases. I do some chores and start chatting to the couple in the camper van "next door." More "Northerners." They are friendly but of the hale and hearty type. Phillippa decided the wife was an ex-teacher and/or a Guide leader. I empty the water tank as the sink was beginning to pong as did the dirty water. I make a note to empty the tank more frequently and vow to get disinfectant to put down the sink.

The rain has returned, so we drive to a huge *supermarché* which seems to sell everything, including disinfectant! We buy a stake and chain for Milo from the pet department. This means we can tether him outside, now the campsites are getting busier and he is not free to roam around. We come to the conclusion that nothing we buy is any cheaper than at home. While we are foraging for goodies, some "kind" French person moved our trolley, whereupon we spent fifteen minutes wandering around in frustration glaring into everyone else's trolley in case they contained our contents (not good for Anglo/French relations!). The thought of having to start shopping again didn't bear thinking about. Eventually, we found our trolley complete with contents; what a relief. On leaving the *intermarché*, we seek out a garage and enquire about a spare tyre/*pneu* for Escargot. We are told to return on Monday (today is Saturday). We drive back to our pitch and pack away the shopping. It is brightening up now. I am feeling a bit "cheesed off" and in need of exercise. I walk Milo down to the lake and walk around it as far as I can. I feel so much better now I am outside breathing in the fresh air. Phillippa has lifted her bike down from the cycle rack for the first time and has gone off for a bike ride.

Today is *Dimanche*. During the night we had some thunder and lightning and more heavy rain. The morning is overcast and chilly. It gradually brightens up and the warmth returns. We decide to walk in the hills behind the site where we discover there are many way- marked paths. We startle a deer and Milo takes off in hot pursuit, but fortunately the deer is too swift for him. Lots of mountain bikers and joggers pass us. They are obviously very into their fitness here in Annecy. We descend through woods to Sevrier. It is really hotting up now. We pass some fabulous property, again very much in the Swiss chalet-style. This is obviously an affluent area. We drop down to Lake Annecy and Milo gets a much-needed swim. We arrive back at the campsite and sit outside for our lunch and watch a couple playing *pétanque*. We study the map and decide to drive around the lake to Menthon-Saint Bernard. We drive up to the amazing Chateau de Menthon, where apparently according to legend, St. Bernard was born. We park up and walk up to Coll de Menthon where there is a pretty village and a church and lots of spring flowers in gardens. Back to Escargot and we continue around the lake to Talloires where we watch paragliders/hang gliders coming down from the Coll and landing. Again, stunning scenery with the lake on one side and mountains beyond. We continue driving around to Duignt and Sevrier and then back to the campsite.

Phillippa goes blading again; this, it seems, has become her evening therapy. I chat to our neighbours "hale and hearty" who have also been walking in the hills today. We had noticed their pristine polished boots outside their van this morning. Our campers from Manchester left to return home earlier in the day. Rob and his mate are staying for a month to continue paragliding. Today has been a good day, much more positive than yesterday – what a difference the sunshine makes.

Phillippa drives Escargot up onto chocks this evening for the first time. It is not an easy manoeuvre at a first attempt as the front wheels need to be aligned with the chocks underneath. Our "hearty" neighbour is quick to give instructions and supervises the procedure with enthusiasm. We are worried about another tyre as it is emitting a hissing noise.

Wake at 7 am and go outside. I cannot believe we have another FLAT tyre; this time at the front of Escargot. "Hail and hearty" turn out to be called Alan and Beryl and yes, we discover, they are both teachers! They are very kind and helpful and fill up our water tank with their hose. Alan seems to think it is just bad luck that we have another flat. We resort to ringing roadside recovery again. The girl who owns the campsite is really sweet and friendly and speaks some English. She introduces us to the chap who runs the campsite shop who can speak English well. The mechanic arrives eventually and with the help of our shop owner "translator" explains the garage will supply us with two new tyres, but he will have to go away and price them. He shows us a nail embedded in the tyre, so it was not anything stupid we had done, it was just something called "sod's law"!

Whilst we wait for the mechanic to return, we sit in the sunshine and read. The site has really thinned out now and we have it more or less to ourselves. There are still two Brits left in a caravan and they come over and make a great fuss of Milo. They ask me about pet passports and what is involved as they want to bring their dog with them next year. The mechanic phones on my mobile and informs me that the tyres are going to cost 300 €.

Gulp. More than I had expected. The mechanic returns at 3 pm and fixes the wheels. We then have to go with him in his car to the garage to settle the bill. He is a really happy chappy; doesn't speak much English but obviously thinks he is Schumacher in his souped-up car. He keeps taking his hands off the wheel and turning around to chat up Phillippa which is somewhat disconcerting! We finally arrive at the garage and I make another phone call to my camper van insurers. I keep getting given conflicting advice as to what I have to pay for (frankly they are not of much help). The lady in the garage is very sweet and speaks a little English. Eventually, I understand I will have to pay for the two tyres and the call out because we didn't have a spare tyre. The final bill is 400€. It is really gutting as we had intended that very morning to go to the garage to get a replacement spare tyre. We are now paranoid about *pneus* and it has made us very dubious about going off-piste away from tarmac roads. We shall definitely have to be on an economy drive from now on. No more coffees out! Our happy mechanic drives us back to the campsite and waves us a cheery goodbye.

Now that Escargot is fully functional, we decide to move on to another campsite at the other end of Lake Annecy. We bid our farewells to the English-speaking chap at the site shop, where we have felt happy and are sad to leave in some ways. It has been very humid all day and now it starts to thunder and absolutely chucks it down with rain. We need petrol so drive into Annecy to a petrol station – definitely not a wise move as it is the rush hour and the traffic is at a standstill with everyone leaning on their horns. My anxiety levels are high. After the *pneu* episodes, I am worried we will have a prang, but thankfully my fears are unfounded. Having filled up with petrol, we carry on in pouring rain to Duingt and find the site, which we have entirely to ourselves. We are both feeling somewhat irritated and stressed. Very relieved to be off the road and parked up. I cook supper. The rain clears and so we take Milo for a much-needed walk along the cycle *piste*. The sky is awesome – misty cloud over the mountains and light coming through on to the lake. The air is so fresh now after the thunder. It is a bit spooky going out to the shower block that night. The site is empty. We go together and take Milo for security to act as a guard dog. I am glad to crawl into bed as I feel shattered after the events of the day.

Later the following morning the weather clears and out comes the sun, hooray! I take my bicycle off the bike rack for the first time and cycle along the *piste*. I feel so liberated and sing to myself as I cycle past lots of red poppies growing in the banks. Phillippa blades with Milo, although dogs are not supposed to be on the track!

We pack up and leave Duingt and drive on towards Cusy. We stop at the top of a mountain road overlooking a valley and have a picnic lunch. A lady on the Annecy site had recommended a campsite in the Beaumont area so that is where we are heading. We pass Aix-les-Bains and go through Grenoble, a large modern city which has 35,000 students, or so "The Lonely Planet" guide tells me. The Belvedere campsite at la Mure lives up to the recommendation. It is well kept and spotlessly clean. I pick up a leaflet of local walks from the reception. We follow one route from the site with Milo in tow, walking through the lanes to the village behind, passing through pretty meadows full of flowers. When we get back to the site, the campsite owner's dog suddenly attacks Milo for no apparent reason. What a commotion there is – fur flying and both dogs apparently biting each other, snarling and snapping, and the French campers shouting and gesticulating, heads popping out of tents and caravans. I was yelling "get him off, get him off" as the *chien* pinned Milo down. I had Euro signs flashing before my eyes as I envisaged a whole month's rent going on vet's fees. Thankfully, there were no injuries. The "he" turned out to be a she called "Prune" who apparently was normally docile and *très gentile*. Prune's owner is very concerned about Milo. She speaks good English and is very sweet. "Don't worry," I say. "It was just a lot of hot air." *Madame* is perplexed. "'ow you say thees 'ot air?" How to explain!? The vagaries of the English language. All was well but we needed a glass or two of wine that evening to calm our nerves.

I decide to have a meal in the little restaurant – I am the only one there. I have jambon omelette and *frites*, not expensive but I still feel guilty spending the money. I enjoy talking to the lady owner who is still concerned about Milo and find out some local information.

We like this campsite; the showers are spotlessly clean. There is a swimming pool, but it's not warm enough to swim. It will be our last day here, so we decide to do another one of the walks in the leaflet. We get a bit lost as cannot find the exact walk. We end up going through lots of different villages, all beautifully kept with neat vegetable gardens and pots of geraniums outside the shuttered windows. Everywhere is seemingly deserted. We get excited when we see two collie puppies on a farm, the first collies we have seen in France. We sit on the step of Escargot and have our lunch looking up at Mount de l'Obiou. We get a bit "ratty" with each other as Phillippa is hormonal. We drive on to Gap in silence, through breath-taking scenery of mountains and valleys. Stop in Gap briefly. It seems a pleasant town and it would have been good to have had time to explore. Going through the town we stop at a zebra crossing and witness a poor old chap knocked down by a lad on a moped. They both landed in a heap. Pedestrians come to the old man's aid and get him to his feet, so we hope he was all right. There was nothing we can do, so we drive on but are quite shaken up by seeing it happen.

We are travelling through much flatter countryside now with lots of fruit trees. I have been disappointed with Provence as I had visualised in my mind's eye fields and fields of lavender, but we are too early in the season for that. Phillippa suggests we pull over into a field where we brew tea and have a snack. I need to go to a bank to draw out more money, so we go into the next town which is Laragne-Montéglin. I have planned the route to take us to the next campsite at Orpierre. Again, this is one I found in the Alan Rogers book. The site is set on a hillside above the village with huge, towering rock faces around. It is renowned as a rock climbing venue. After supper, we walk into Orpierre. Seemingly deserted. The little town dates back to Medieval times and the houses have hardly changed with narrow, cobbled streets surrounded by the craggy rock faces. I find it fascinating; it reminds me of how I would imagine a Mexican town to look. Definitely a perfect location for a film set... straight out of "A Fistful of Dollars." Suddenly, Milo starts sniffing and whining at the door of one of the shuttered houses. We stop and listen and can hear a cat mewing and scratching pitifully behind the door. Phillippa is really concerned as she thinks the cat could be trapped and starving. We go off and try and find somebody in the vicinity. Fortunately, we meet an English-speaking chap who, it transpires, works as a chef in the nearby gites.

He comes back with us to where we heard the cat mewing. He assures us that said pussy is not trapped and that somebody does live in the house.

Back at our site, we get talking to a Welsh couple whose camper is parked next to ours. They help us position Escargot on the chocks to get it level. "Mrs Welsh" thinks Phillippa and I are friends and doesn't believe I am her mother. It makes my day of course!

We do seem to cause quite a stir when we arrive on campsites. It was very unusual at that time to see two women driving a camper van, especially a mother aged fifty-two and her twenty-four- year-old daughter, accompanied by their dog. The men on the sites loved to give us advice on the intricacies of camping and where we were going wrong! (Not that we thought we were, but we liked to humour them.) After a few weeks, Phillippa became an expert at reversing Escargot onto a pitch, and we became adept at hooking up to the electricity supply.

We wake to another hot and sunny day. Have a leisurely start and sit outside for breakfast. I leave Phillippa reading and stroll down into Orpierre with Milo. I wander around taking lots of photographs. I really love this place for some reason and have an affinity with it. Perhaps it is because it is steeped in history dating back to AD 500, but also because it does have a certain peace and serenity about its deserted streets. Apparently, only about thirty villagers still live here all the year round; the remaining houses are let out as gites in the summer.

Orpierre only has about one hour of sun in the winter months and therefore is very cold. I don't think I shall be moving here as I couldn't cope with so little sunshine in winter.

I meet Phillippa in the *pétanque* square where we sit outside a café enjoying two cold beers as we watch groups of rock climbers scaling the rock faces.

We pack up and leave Orpierre and drive on to Volonne in Provence. Our next campsite is a large one by a lake and has a swimming pool. It is still only May and so fairly quiet. I wouldn't want to be here in the height of summer when I would imagine it would be extremely busy. The sun is starting to heat up, and we put our awning up for the first time and have our supper outside. We walk Milo by the lake and he has lots of swims, then carry on walking into Volonne itself. It is a typical Provence village with lots of narrow streets and tall houses with balconies festooned with red geraniums.

For the first time that night, we actually feel warm in bed instead of chilly. The day dawns and brings hot sunshine. We are in Provence after all, and we are now halfway between Gap and Antibes. We walk into Volonne once more and visit the market. It is not terribly exciting, but we do buy some gorgeous cherries (cerise) and homemade pizza from a van. Back on site, we sit outside Escargot and gorge ourselves on cherries. The campsite itself has lots of cherry trees growing and the fruit is ripening with some falling on to the ground.

I take a pile of washing to put in the site washing machine and start chatting to a lovely Dutch couple who tell me that they are retired but are living and working on the site for three months. Like all the Dutch people we have met thus far, they prove to be very friendly and welcoming.

We spot a GB sticker on a camper van and greet the occupants; a couple in their thirties called Janine and Ralph who we learn are doing a similar thing to us. They too bought a camper van, have let out their house in Warwick and are travelling around France until September. They tell us that they are finding everything far more expensive than they had envisaged and are spending above their budget, which helps me feel a bit better in a peculiar sort of way. Janine and Ralph come across to see us later and we sit under the awning (it is very hot). We learn that they are on their way up from the South and so are able to give us some good tips and recommendations of sites to stay on once we get there. We have a pleasant evening with them; they are a very chatty couple, and it is good for Phillippa to meet people who are more her age group.

It is now so hot that we take advantage of the open air pool and go for a swim. Fabulous! It is so refreshing. We really enjoy ourselves. Poor old Milo – we let him swim in the lake to cool off. Ralph kindly brings us over a bag of cherries he and Janine have picked from the trees. We decide to pick some ourselves too – well, they are free. A really sweet French couple who see us struggling with our awning pole to reach the branches of the trees come and give us a dishful of cherries and then help us pick some from a tree next to their caravan.

The days are getting hotter, and we are so glad of the swimming pool and the lake for Milo to swim in. We are now settling into life in Escargot. It is amazing how the days go by.

Phillippa is glad of her bunk aloft with the curtain as it gives her privacy and space from me. After breakfast she usually washes up whilst I empty the loo at the designated sluice. We try and keep the van as tidy as possible. Milo is long haired and sheds his fur in the van. We have a stiff wire brush which we use on the carpet to try and get the hair up. Most mornings, one of us gives Milo a brush and comb outside to get rid as much of his fur as we can. He absolutely loves this and the attention he receives. Lunch now consists of a cheese (*fromage*) and tomato (*tomate*) baguette every day which I cut in half and put in the fridge for the next day. It can be a bit chewy second time around, but I am on an economy drive. Our supper is preceded by olives and sometimes sun-dried tomatoes and a glass of Côte du Rhône red wine. We have discovered this to be the cheapest brand in the *supermarchés*. For supper we usually have a salad and jambon or hard-boiled eggs and sardines or whatever veg is cheapest, invariably followed by fruit or yoghurt. Not exactly haute cuisine.

We do get space from one another during the day, by the time one goes to the wash up to do the dishes or the shower block for personal hygiene whilst the other walks Milo or tidies up Escargot. We usually have emails to read or write and I write a lot of postcards. Added expense with postage but the need to remain in contact with people is very strong. Those who have experienced bereavement will understand the sense of aloneness and insecurity that it brings and the need to have affirmation of friendship and love. I also write my travel blog every day, and all this takes time. So, our days go by and we fall into some sort of routine.

It is now the 24th May and we are enjoying relaxing in the sunshine and not having to move on. We are out of provisions, however, and so drive to a local *intermarché* to stock up. We have learnt now to leave our picnic chairs and table on our pitch and sometimes washing hanging out, otherwise some new arrival could come and drive onto our pitch. Once back on our spot, we sit outside for our picnic lunch and read. Later, we head to the pool for a deliciously refreshing swim. Milo now spends most of the day inside Escargot, where it is cooler, apart from regular trips to the lake for swims.

We are not yet aware that 2003 will be one of the hottest summers on record and we have no air conditioning in Escargot. The warmth we are experiencing now is nothing to how it will become later on.

Dimanche: We are on the move once more. We say our farewells to Ralph and Janine and exchange email addresses. We are sad to be parting from them, but this is how it is with travelling around. We have decided to head on towards Digne-les-Bains on the N85 and then to Castellane. The road proves to be very twisty with hairpin bends and sheer drops down to gorges below. We are in need of a break so stop at a terraced cafe and treat ourselves to the *plat du jour*, which turns out to be quite fatty pork chops with boiled potatoes covered in a delicious dressing of olive oil, parsley and garlic with a small salad, followed by a glacé. It is a refreshing change to eat out and enjoy some traditional French cooking. Our campsite turns out to be a large one, fortunately not too busy as it is still low season. A young German couple camp next to us with their little boy Felix and their Jack Russell dog called Nino. Milo and Nino hit it off immediately and spend a lot of time playing together. Phillippa decides to have a swim in the pool, but it is unheated and freezing, far too cold for me. Instead, I walk Milo around the campsite to orientate myself and find a designated footpath into Castellane which I take. En route I meet another German couple who make a big fuss of Milo; he is certainly a conversation opener. In Castellane there is a funfair in the main square. I wander off around the narrow back streets which are very similar to Volonne with tall, shuttered houses with balconies.

Surprisingly, the next morning we awake to pouring rain and so stay in bed and read. We pack up late morning – it is still raining but not so heavily. Quite a few of our fellow campers had told us about the Gorges du Verdon, a well-known attraction nearby. We plan to drive around it. Not a good move it later transpires. It is a spectacular gorge with a river running through miles below the sheering cliffs. The road is steep, windy and hairy in places with terrifying drops on one side. There are various stopping places along the route to enable drivers to admire the views. It's stopped raining thankfully. The twisty road climbs up to the pretty village of Moustiers-Saint-Marie. We are glad to park up and stretch our legs. There are lots of gift shops selling rather tacky ornate china. Milo appreciates the circular walk around the village. There is an abundance of yellow gorse which has a heady perfume.

Needless to say, Phillippa does the driving around the gorge. I am full of admiration. The road seems to go on and on. I am starting to think we are never going to come out the other side. It is like a maze: once in, we have to continue to find our way out. The ending of the film "Thelma and Louise" comes into my mind; one false move and we are done for. I spend a lot of the time praying for safety. Poor Milo is not at all happy about being thrown around and is getting distressed, until he suddenly jumps into the front with me which is highly dangerous. I clamber over the passenger seat to the back of the van and persuade him to join me. All the while there is the clattering of saucepans, and the colander which is hanging above us falls off, which alarms Milo even more. The doors of the overhead cupboards fly open. I stroke Milo and try to calm him. I really feel for Phillippa who I can see is getting tired and stressed with the concentration. We are starting to feel sick. Finally, with relief we emerge from the gorge. We have definitely seen enough of gorges of any description for some time.

Exhausted, we arrive at our campsite on the outskirts of Grasse at 7 pm. I make a hurried supper and then give Milo a walk along a lane behind the campsite; he deserves a good walk, poor chap, after his rotten day. It is a relief to be out in the fresh air after being in Escargot for so long. I feel we are both fed up after today and are glad to go to bed early.

Still a slight drizzle but a better morning. I do the same walk with Phillippa as last evening, but we walk further this time and have a good gawp at the fabulous property and gardens, some with swimming pools, most with security gates. We love the terracotta tiled roofs and the orchards of lemon and orange trees. We are both feeling much more positive today. One of the highlights of this campsite is the wash up. It is situated outside with the sinks overlooking a spectacular view. Washing up is less of a chore and takes longer as it is tempting just to stand and stare. Why not?!

We drive into Grasse, famous for its perfume, where we park up and walk around the pleasant town. We would have enjoyed going on a tour of the perfumery, but it costs money and we have Milo in tow.

Ralph and Janine had recommended a campsite at Mandelieu-la-Napoule, near Cannes. It is definitely the best we have stayed on thus far – spotlessly clean, set amongst pine trees with a sun trap of a swimming pool. Each pitch is on gravel surrounded by little privet hedges which give privacy and a certain amount of seclusion. It is small with only twenty pitches for mobile homes. It is hard to imagine that such a quiet, peaceful site is in the middle of a busy town. We are right alongside the Siagne canal too, which is brilliant for Milo as he can have lots of swims. We decide to stay three days. It is so relaxing here although a tad expensive.

Phillippa decides to spring clean Escargot whilst I walk Milo along the canal and enjoy watching people in their boats and give them a wave. We sit outside again on our little pitch and eat our supper. A family walks past and wishes us "*Bon appetit.*" At the wash up afterwards I get chatting to a family from Wales. They are only here for just over a week and it took them twenty-four hours to drive from Calais. They come over to Escargot and make a fuss of Milo and ask us lots of questions about our trip.

Today, 29th May, would have been our wedding anniversary. Phillippa and I have our breakfast outside in the sunshine. I love the smell of the pine trees and hearing the magpies chattering.

We give Milo his walk by the canal. At 9.30 am it is already hot. It is a Bank Holiday in France for Ascension Day. We are going to visit Cannes today which gives us an excuse to dress up a bit and put on some makeup. We leave Milo locked in Escargot with windows open. It will be nice and cool for him. We walk to the bus stop and catch the 602 bus into Cannes. We feel quite excited. It makes a pleasant change not to have to drive and park the van and worry about Milo.

We walk around the marina and admire all the fabulous yachts with their liveried crew. A film crew are filming a girl gyrating to pop music on one of the yachts. We see the famous Cannes Film Festival building, but it doesn't look that impressive without the red carpet and glittering celebrities outside. Phillippa treats me to lunch at a pleasant restaurant. We sit outside and watch the world go by. I have the *plat du jour* of veal (which I wouldn't normally eat on principle) but it was *très bon* and the sauce was wonderful. We share a carafe of rosé. It is hard not to think that I should be sitting here with my husband celebrating our anniversary, but I am so grateful that I am with Phillippa, so thankful that I am in France and all this is a huge distraction.

Overall we are not that impressed with Cannes. Parts of it, away from the marina, we found quite sleazy. At least we can say we have been there. We catch the bus back to the site.

Poor Milo has been left in Escargot for six hours. We feel really guilty. Dear Milo, he has been so good. We try and make it up to him. An English lady tells us how to get to the marina and *plage* in La Napoule. We walk Milo along a river, where he enjoys copious swims, and arrive at the marina. We walk across the *plage* underneath a castle/chateau built in the 1930s by an American. We start chatting to an English guy with a golden retriever who has lived here for two years. Before that, he lived in Switzerland. He tells us he runs an "Irish" bar in La Napoule. We walk the same route back to the site and fall into bed, really tired after our exciting day out.

The hot, sunny weather continues. Milo has his usual walk by the canal. We do the necessary chores, empty the tank, fill up with water etc. ready to leave and say our goodbyes to our dear little Welsh family. Next stop, Antibes. En route we stop at an *intermarché* and stock up with food once again. Our campsite is at Villeneuve Loubet Plage between Antibes and Nice. It has a fabulous open air pool, and we both spend a lot of time enjoying swimming and cooling off. As it is still only May the campsites are never too full, and we can have the privilege of using almost empty swimming pools. Wonderful. Supper is al fresco once more. Afterwards, we walk Milo in a large park adjoining the campsite called Vaugrenier Park. It reminds me of the common near my village at home, with lots of trees and paths. Milo absolutely loves it; it makes a change for him to have open countryside to run and hunt in.

Today is Saturday (*Samedi*) and there are hordes of joggers out this morning when we walk Milo in the park. We are walking earlier now as it gets very hot later in the day. I drove Phillippa mad last evening by lying on my bed reciting over and over the days of the week in French. She yanked her curtain back above and said, "Mum shut up! I'm trying to read!" We drive to Antibes and manage to park on the outskirts next to a football ground from whence we walk into the resort past the marina, which is full of expensive yachts.

Awesome. We pass under an arch which leads into the old town. There is a huge covered market selling all kinds of produce; it's bustling with people. We buy some olives, salad, aubergine and artichokes. We wander in the cool of the old streets and sit outside a café and have beers and a *croque monsieur*. Whilst we are enjoying our lunch, a group of accordionists and a saxophonist serenade us. It gives us a good feeling. We walk to the beach so that Milo can swim. It is very hot and keeping him cool is essential. We limp back to Escargot feeling somewhat wilted. Back at the campsite, we head straight for the pool and relish in a refreshing swim. Early evening I go to the camp office to use their internet and try and access my current account, but after much futile effort discover I need a code so it's a waste of time.

Dimanche: 1st June. We have been in France a month already. I found out at the site office that there is an International Church in Cannes. We decide to go. Holy Trinity Church is an impressive building. We are a bit disappointed as had hoped to connect with some local people. The congregation are mainly older although there is a children's talk for the few children there. It seems a lot of people have come from the big cruise liners moored off Cannes. Some of the ladies are very chic and glamorous. I feel a right scruff bag in my camper van gear. We mingle in the coffee lounge where wine is served as well as coffee.

This is France after all! I We start talking to a sweet couple who are retired doctors and own a holiday villa up in the hills. They live in Exeter, my local city at home, and it turns out they know one of my neighbours, also a doctor, very well. It certainly is a small world. It is still hot when we leave church so manage to drive and park at the end of the seafront. Phillippa blades with Milo whilst I sit on a seat and people-watch.

Back to site for a much-needed swim. We both agree that we much prefer Antibes to Cannes.

Milo is becoming Trog like and spends a great deal of time lying under the van where it is cool. It is amazing how many French people recognise him as a border collie. We have not seen any here at all apart from the puppies we saw on a farm way back in the mountains. The French love their *chiens* but unlike in England where every other dog seems to be a collie or at least half of one, they don't seem to keep them as pets here. But on seeing Milo they will say (and this has to be said with a heavy French accent), "Ah, Border collie, *oui*?" and make a great fuss of him. I was chatting to a German chap on one site who told me they have a version of "One Man and his Dog" on German television, so perhaps the same applies to the French. I have come to the conclusion that they must all watch it avidly as one man asked us if we kept sheep!

Today is a big day. We are going to Monte Carlo. We walk

to Biot railway station and catch a train to Monte Carlo. That evening we are told will see the start of a forty eight hour strike. The French it appears are always on strike for something. As a result the train is jam- packed. This has to be the hottest day we have had thus far, and Milo is feeling the heat.

We cannot believe we are actually in famous Monte Carlo. The Grand Prix finished last weekend and the scaffolding and stands are still in situ. We walk to the renowned casino and stand and stare in awe at all the posh cars; Ferraris, Lamborghinis, Porches and Bentleys. The drivers, hiding behind their dark shades, hop out and toss their keys to waiting liveried porters who park the cars for them. It is another world. We would love to have been able to go inside the casino, but this is out of the question. We walk up the slope to the Palace of the Grimaldi family and enjoy spectacular views over the harbour (again filled with state-of-the-art yachts,) and out over the bay. We visit the magnificent cathedral which is an impressive monument of white stone and inside see the tomb where Princess Grace is buried. We wander down little streets full of "Grand Prix" gifts – all a bit tacky. Walk back through the gardens taking in views and are in awe of the property with their rooftop gardens and private swimming pools. We even see a helicopter land on one property's own helicopter pad. Monte Carlo really is the most incredible place; the height of decadence and wealth. I have difficulty in dragging Phillippa past the exclusive shops: Prada, Gucci, Yves St. Laurent and Dior – her favourite fashion label – gulp! We return to the station and catch a double-decker train back to Biot. It feels strange going upstairs on a train. Milo is so good; he huddles up against my legs; it is so hot. We have fabulous views of the coastline and sparkling blue sea. As soon as we disembark at Biot, we let Milo go in for a swim. We walk him back to the campsite, a quick supper and shower before bed as we feel so hot and sticky.

Our last day on this site. We pack up once more and drive along the coast road between Antibes and Nice. We stop by a pebbly beach and have a picnic. We lie and sunbathe and read, followed by a swim along with Milo who just swims and swims; he loves it. En route to La Colle Sur Loop, we pull into a *supermarché* for more provisions. Our campsite, Les Pinedes, as its name implies, is set amongst pine trees and has a superb pool. Due to the unusually hot weather, even for early June, my priority now is to find a site with shade and that almost essential swimming pool. Once pitched up, we have supper and walk Milo by the river. Back on site, we get chatting to an English girl, in her thirties, called Elouise who has a black Labrador called Phoebe. She invites us back to her camper for a glass of wine, where we meet her husband Tim who is recovering from an accident. He had come off his mountain bike (that particular day he did not bother to wear a helmet), knocked himself out and had narrowly missed being run over by a car, and had spent a few days in hospital in Antibes. Their camper van is a Fiat Royale like ours but a bigger version, and they are also travelling for three and a half months and are planning to return on the 15th August (as are we). Even Phoebe, their dog, is the same age as Milo. How amazing is that! They are the first people we have met who have brought their dog with them from England. Milo is delighted to meet another English dog to converse with! The cooling system had gone on their van and had to be taken to a garage. It sounded expensive. As a result, they had been on the site for over two weeks recovering.

At Les Pinedes, for three weeks from the end of May and into June, the evenings are alive with firefly (glow worms) lighting up the site. We feel very privileged to be here at this time of year to be able to witness the display. That evening, I walk Milo up to the top of the site and I'm mesmerised by the fireflies. They are an incredible sight; it is akin to watching tiny strobe lights flicking on and off. It is a beautiful, warm, balmy evening. Couples are sitting out with little candles on their tables with the fireflies all around. It is all rather romantic and how I wish I had my husband to share it with. I sit outside Escargot for a while reflecting on my loss. Phillippa has gone to bed.

Another really hot day. It has become the norm now. We discover a lovely walk through a gorge by a river where Milo can swim to his heart's content. Walking back along a busy road, a car stops in front of us. A lady gets out and starts talking to us in French, until she discovers we are English. She is very friendly and wants to know where we had got Milo from, thinking he had come from a breeder in France. It transpires she is English and has lived here for ten years but has never seen a border collie in this region during that time. She had always wanted a border collie. I think if we had named our price she would happily have taken Milo with her – but he is NOT for sale.

I do two machine loads of washing, and we rig up a clothes line between trees and hang it out to dry. We head up into the hills to the medieval walled town of St. Paul de Venice.

Apparently, Roger Moor has a home here. Alas, we don't bump into him at all. St Paul is very quaint with narrow streets full of artists' studios and gift shops. It is rather commercialised and full of Americans. It had a certain charm though, and I could understand why Roger would buy a property here. On our return, we discover Milo has peed on the carpet in Escargot and it stinks. Phillippa gives it a good scrubbing. It's just too hot to do much, so we swim in the *piscine* and then sunbathe and read. Whilst swimming, Phillippa got talking to a young English couple. She invites them around for a drink after supper. Dave and Amy are in their early twenties, so it is good for Phillippa to have someone of her own age group to hang out with. They are a lovely young couple – really nice, open and friendly. They tell us that they have been travelling using a tent since March and had planned to stay in France until November but were running out of money and like us, also planned to return home in August. They give us the names of some interesting places to visit further south and write down the campsite locations. It transpires Dave is a mechanic by trade and is able to show Phillippa how to change the oil in Escargot. Later that night, I walk up with Phillippa to the top of the site to see the fireflies again. She is as enthralled as I am and keeps saying, "Wow Mum, this is amazing!" Amazing is one of her favourite words.

We are on the move once more and pack up and give

Escargot a thorough clean. I fill up with water. We drive to the river gorge to give Milo a walk and swim and then drive on to Cap d'Antibes. How exotic does that sound? We drive around the stunning peninsular and strain our necks to catch glimpses of some of the exclusive villas where the rich and famous abound (Tina Turner being one such celebrity) and that are hidden behind high walls and electronic gates. Talk about being barricaded in. Cars (let alone camper vans) are not encouraged to park – signs of being clamped and towed away are everywhere. We know our place, so we stop our humble, dear Escargot by a river and have a picnic lunch. More swims for Milo. Carry on to Fréjus Saint-Aygulf. We check out a couple of campsites, but both are big and crowded so decide to carry on towards Saint-Tropez. Did I really just say that: Saint-Tropez?! Or San Trop as they call it here, dahling! I locate a campsite right on the beach. It is expensive but we decide for one night we can treat ourselves. The proprietor turns out to be a canny Scot. We have a bit of banter with him. He tells us that the "Beckhams" (who?!) have recently bought a property nearby. The location is pretty awesome, right beside the Mediterranean looking across to Saint-Tropez. Awesome. We savour the moment and walk along the beach where Milo has his usual swims. Is he aware, I wonder, that this time he is swimming in the Med?

Our sleep that night is somewhat disturbed by noisy traffic – we are on the busy coast road. It is something else, however, to be able to walk out of Escargot first thing in the morning and be swimming in the Mediterranean Sea before breakfast. Wow.

Whilst having our breakfast, we chat to a retired couple from Somerset who have an enormous camper van parked up on the beach near us. Escargot looks minute alongside. Reluctantly, we have to pack up and leave. We have to visit Saint-Tropez now we are so close. We have been warned by other campers that there are gypsy travellers around who break into vehicles and so are concerned about leaving Escargot. On the approach to Saint-Tropez, we find a spot on the side of a road where other cars are parked. Phillippa expertly parks tight against a wall. We pull all the blinds down in the van and make sure we take any valuables with us, and I treble check that everything is locked and as secure as can be. It is hotter than ever today,. Poor Milo, he is feeling the heat with all his fur. We walk into Saint-Tropez. I was half expecting it to be really commercial. We were pleasantly surprised; it is a pretty little village with oodles of charm. We love the colour of the houses, painted in bright Mediterranean colours. We wander around the marina and find we are becoming almost blasé now at the sight of luxury yachts. The shops and market are expensive but we both really like it here. Just as well we can't stay too long. We weren't going to spend any money but as it is so hot, we sit outside a café in the shade and order two beers. The atmosphere is friendly and relaxing. We head back to Escargot and are very relieved to find him safe and sound.

We take the D559 and drive up above the coast road to the Le Cros de Mouton campsite which is set amongst pine trees with views over the bay. The first thing we do is head for the *piscine* for a long swim. When it cools down in the evening, we walk Milo along a quiet road up in the hills.

We are out of touch with what is happening in the world – is there something going down in Holland? – the country must be empty because it seems the campsites are full of Dutch talking ' double Dutch ' to each other.

A fairly relaxing morning and then drive back along the fabulous stretch of coast road, with the shimmering Mediterranean on one side with beaches and bobbing boats and attractive pan-tiled villas on the other. The roads are busy as it is *Dimanche* and everyone, it seems, has flocked to the beach.

We are going to visit Hyères which was recommended to Phillippa by a work colleague. We drive along the peninsula to Giens where there is a campsite right at the end, but it is heaving and everyone is packed in like sardines. We can't hack that so carry on to the one listed in the Alan Rogers book at Carqueiranne about 8 km from Hyères. We badly need to stock up on provisions but being *Dimanche,* the shops are closed. We like the Beau Veze site; it is quiet and amongst pine trees. It also has a great pool to swim and relax in. Our "neighbours" in a camper van are Belgian and seem very friendly but don't speak English. That evening we download and read our emails; it always cheers us up to get news from home.

The next morning, the Belgian couple knock on our door and make it clear that Milo has done his jobbies on their pitch. I clear it up and apologise but it is all rather embarrassing. We are feeling somewhat hemmed in so decide to move on. We pass a fruit and veg stall and stop and buy some produce. We drive into Hyères (pronounced e air) which is renowned for its date palms which grow in and around the town. They are even exported to Arab palaces evidently. The old town with its wide streets and palms is how I imagine a town in Saudi Arabia to look. It is very hot and uncomfortable to walk around in. We have a picnic lunch under the awning of Escargot. We have discovered that today is a Bank Holiday. We drive to a *supermarché* but as we suspected it is shut, which is a pain as we are out of supplies. We drive down the peninsula looking for a beach but unfortunately along this stretch, *chiens* are forbidden on the *plage*. Because it is a Bank Holiday there are lots of cars and people everywhere. After a couple of failed attempts, we manage to find a campsite which is quiet and laid back. I am trying not to use the Alan Rogers book now because the sites are excellent but proving expensive. It does mean, however, that it takes us more time to look for a site. On arrival we seem to cause quite a stir, and it is quite funny as two or three French campers delight in directing Phillippa on to the correct pitch. We leave Milo in the van as it is too hot to walk him, but we go to the beach which is only a short stroll away down a track. It is exhilarating to swim in the sea – so refreshing. My swimming is coming on in leaps and bounds. Lie on the beach and read. That evening we treat ourselves to supper at the little camp café. We have pizza and salad. We really enjoy it – quite a chilled atmosphere. It is a beautiful evening, so warm and balmy; the colours of the sea and sky are fantastic. We walk Milo across the beach and over the cliff path. It's such a romantic setting, my heart aches; I long to have my husband here to share it with.

We had planned to go over to Ile de Porquerolles today, but we just want to relax and don't wake up very early. This is such a cool site, a bit scruffy and casual but is has a good feel to it. We like the bamboos growing all around. I do love waking up on different sites each morning and lying looking at the trees. Here we are nice and shaded, and the leaves are so cool and green. The magpies are really noisy in the mornings and chatter away. We walk Milo on the beach and he has lots of swims, but the sea water keeps making him sick and gives him the "runs." Great! We have most of our meals now sitting under the awning in the shade. We have a young German couple in a tent next to us who are into windsurfing. They speak English and enjoy chatting to us.

We leave Milo in the cool of the van and spend the afternoon on the beach, reading, swimming and dozing. Wonderful. Another beautiful evening with a fabulous sunset, and Milo has his walk on the beach. It is still hot at night, so we have taken to chaining Milo up and he sleeps under the van. It is too hot for him and us inside. Was it really only a few weeks ago that we were in Chamonix shivering in our fleeces?

Up and about at 7 am. Pack up a picnic lunch and load up rucksack. Drive to ferry crossing at end of peninsula and pay 9€ to park Escargot in the car park, but at least we know it is safe and guarded. Catch the 10 am ferry across to Ile de Porquerolles. It costs 14€ each so an expensive day out. Milo goes free! It takes less than twenty minutes to reach the island. We set off and walk around some of it. It reminds me of the

Scilly Isles with pine trees coming down to white sandy beaches and clear turquoise sea. Yachts have moored off the little bays and people have come ashore in tenders. We settle on the Plage Notre Dame and swim topless, which feels very liberating. The sea is so warm; it is fabulous. Milo swims with us. We picnic on the beach and sunbathe. Overdo the sun and get quite burnt. I am worried about Milo overheating, so we walk back through the centre of the island under the cool of the pine trees. We see a lot of people on hired bikes cycling around the island. We sit outside a cafe in Le Village and have a can of orange. We are so thirsty and have consumed most of our water. I find a pump which Milo drinks straight from. Poor chap, he was gagging for a drink. He has been sick again and has the squits – the salt water doesn't do him any good. We catch the 5 pm ferry back to the mainland. We have definitely overdone the sun. It is a relief not to have to walk Milo again that evening. He sleeps under the van again, exhausted.

We decide to stay on the site and chill this morning. We catch up on emails, washing and writing up journals. Milo is happy to lie under the van – it really is too hot for him. Phillippa goes off to the beach and a late afternoon swim. I have had enough sun for the time being and am happy to sit under the awning and read and doze. Later I empty the water tank and sweep the floor which is covered with grass. After supper, we give Milo a good walk along the beach and cliff paths. Yet another glorious sunset. When I come back from my evening ablutions, I am somewhat taken aback to find the site caretaker sitting in Escargot chatting to Phillippa. We had sort of befriended him and felt sorry for him as he was obviously not the "sharpest knife in the drawer." It turns out he is from Tunisia and wants us to go there with him for a holiday! I think it's Phillippa he wants to go actually, not me, but in either case it's not going to happen! He is very sad that we are leaving tomorrow.

Yet another hot, sunny day. Milo has an early walk on the beach and over the cliff paths. We pack up and say Auf Wiedersehen to our German neighbour in the tent. He wants to know if Phillippa is a model because he is convinced he has seen her in a Calvin Klein advert. I don't enlighten him to the fact that she has done some modelling in the past but certainly not for Calvin Klein.

We are moving on now to Aix-en-Provence but have to stop off at a *supermarché* once again to stock up. It is stiflingly hot in Escargot even with all the windows open. How we long for air conditioning! I manage to find a campsite easily which is a relief as it is too hot to drive around looking for one and uses up unnecessary fuel. It proves to be a lovely site shaded by lots of trees and only 2km from Aix. Most importantly, it has a *piscine*, which has now become essential. It is the longest pool we have had so far, and we are soon swimming up and down. It's such a relief to cool off and the pool is almost empty. Pure Heaven. Later we find a lovely, shaded river walk under trees which is perfect for Milo.

People are jogging and walking their *chiens*. It really is the perfect spot. When we are eating our supper under the awning, we get chatting to other campers who delight in telling us that this is the hottest June in France for over fifty years and that today it reached 35 degrees Fahrenheit. No wonder we are wilting.

It is becoming increasingly hard to sleep at night because of the heat, even though we don't bother with any bedcovers and have every aperture possible open. Dear Milo has taken up permanent residence under the van. We discover that the shower facilities here are the best we have had thus far: little cubicles with a shower, toilet and basin embellished with pretty blue mosaic tiles. It feels like having one's own en suite. We give Milo an early morning walk along the river and then leave him in Escargot with all the windows open and a big bowl of water. We catch the No. 3 bus into Aix en Provence which is the old capital of Provence. "The Rough Guide" describes it as stunningly beautiful. Well, it is certainly lovely with attractive buildings and squares and a large market. It has a relaxed atmosphere, and we stroll along the famous Le Cours Mirabeau, a wide avenue built for horse and carriages where there are many pavement cafés. We are happy to sit at one and have a couple of beers and enjoy watching the world go by. This is a university town and swarming with students. We have wandered quite far and can't remember how to get back to the bus station. Phillippa stops a young student and asks for directions. He tells us his name is Fabian and kindly offers to walk us back across the town to our bus stop. He speaks excellent English and is studying History. I can't help thinking to myself wryly whether he would have been so keen to enact this good deed if it had just been me on my own. I have soon realised that I am "invisible" when I am accompanied by Phillippa. We catch the bus back to our site. Milo is fine but delighted to see us. I was a bit "naughty" and rather extravagantly bought *The Telegraph*

Milo swimming in the Rhône (a change from the Med)

*Campsite near Sarlat in
Dordogne, sandy/pebble
beach by river.*

*Original Rembrandt,
dated 1611, put 2€ in
slot to light up*

*It feels like being in
the Sahara desert*

Milo trying to remember where he buried his stick !

*Have a meal at this beach side cafe one evening at Notre-Dame de Mont,
on the Vendee*

Miles of Plage along the Atlantic coast on the Vendee - popular for sand surfing/wind sailing

Mornac-sur-Seudre supposedly one of France's prettiest villages

Inside 'Escargot' our home for three and half months

Another view from my 'bedroom' window, this time at a site near St Gilles-Croix-de-Vie

A view of our neighbours from under the awning

newspaper when in Aix. I sit under the awning and read it from cover to cover and thoroughly enjoy every moment, I am so hungry for news from home. We have a refreshing swim in the *piscine* and then whilst preparing supper, start chatting to a chap on the pitch next to ours.

His name is Iain, he is Scottish and tells us he has been coming to this particular campsite for years. He lives in Canada but spends four to five months here each year. He was widowed many years ago and used to teach French. We learn a lot about the area from him. Later we give Milo his usual evening river walk.

It is hot and humid already, even Milo's early morning walk leaves us dripping. We can hear cicada chirruping in the trees all the time but never actually see any, until one, which has burst from its cocoon, perches on our hook-up. It is so exciting that I take a photograph. I have another chat with Iain who actually lives on Nova Scotia and has been on his own for fourteen years. He wishes us well on our travels.

We are heading inland again towards Carpentras. We make a picnic stop by a river so Milo can have his swim. We have started referring to ourselves as "The Three Musketeers." We three are united – Phillippa, me and Milo. We drive on up to Vaison-la-Romaine, the location of our next campsite. We are very much back into rural Provence now: vineyards and fields of sunflowers which are just beginning to open up. Our campsite is high up, surrounded by vineyards with mountain ranges in the distance. The most famous is Mount Ventoux which has large aerials and TV satellites on the top and is one of the most arduous parts of the Tour de France. Once pitched up, we head straight for the *piscine* which is an unusual shape and has "islands" in the middle. It is in a fabulous location, and as we swim round we look out across fields to the mountains. Next our usual frugal supper and glass of wine, after which we walk Milo down a lane through vineyards towards a village. It is so quiet here, again I ponder where do all the French go? We hear some thunder rumbling in the distance and the sound of crickets chirping everywhere.

I don't sleep very well again; it is so humid even with the top of the door open. Not a good start to the day as we discover the fridge is not working. We check everything and even get the site owner to make sure the hook-up is functioning. We drive to the nearby town of Vaison-la-Romaine which has an old, walled medieval part. We mooch around the Roman remains and go into the cathedral which is playing Taizé-type music. Today is Father's Day and Phillippa lights a candle in memory of her dad. I find this very moving and the whole atmosphere is so peaceful, that we certainly feel God's presence. We cross the Roman bridge over the river to the old town. It is fascinating – not unlike St. Paul de Venice but far nicer as not so commercialised. Narrow, cobbled streets with squares and fountains and lots of potted flowers. Back in the relative cool of Escargot, we have a much-needed nap. We have to pop into a *supermarché* on the way back to the site to buy more juice, water and milk. I am quite concerned about the fridge as it is still not working. What will we do if it has packed up in this heat? We go for a swim as usual, desperate to cool off. I decide to ditch the food in the fridge as the fromage has gone off, and I don't feel it is worth risking the jambon and yoghurt. Phillippa finds the handbook for the fridge which says it should be kept level. We had been on a definite tilt. Phillippa drives Escargot up on to the chocks.

When we come back later from giving Milo his walk, we discover the fridge is working. What a relief. A pity we had not checked the handbook before, but we live and learn as they say.

A really sweet French couple are camping next door and make a great fuss of Milo and keep asking, "*Très gente, très gente, oui?*" I reply, "*Oui, oui très gente.*"

We do the usual chores in the van ready for moving on. Have one last swim in the *piscine* which we have all to ourselves which is absolutely wonderful. Bid "au revoir" to our French neighbours, who make a great show of bidding Milo farewell… "*Ah très gente, très gente,*" they croon. I think they are sad to see him go.

Next stop, Orange. I irritate Phillippa because I keep saying it's not pronounced orange as in fruit but say in my best French accent it is "Or an je." We find a shady spot in the car park and leave Milo in the van whilst we go to visit the Roman amphitheatre. We do the whole tourist thing and walk around with audio guides clamped to our ears with an English commentary. It is fascinating and amazing to think it has survived all these years. It has to be the hottest day ever. We are baking sitting on the tiered seats. Apparently, in Roman times, they had a huge canvas awning which they stretched across the spectator's seats – clever lot those Romans. What a pity it's not in situ today.

It is too hot to walk, so we make the decision to drive on to Montpellier with a view to staying on a site in between. However, my navigational skills are not up to scratch today and we have lost our direction. Phillippa gets a bit ratty with me. Understandably, she is hot and tired of driving, and says with exasperation, "Mum I can't drive and navigate at the same time!" We end up in Avignon. I have redeemed myself by finding a campsite just outside of the city walls by the River Rhône from whence we can walk into the town.

Avignon looks spectacular with its walled ramparts and gold statue glinting in the evening sun. The campsite named du Pont d'Avignon is in fact on an island between two stretches of the Rhône river. We love the wide pitches shaded by trees.

It starts to thunder, and we actually have some rain although it doesn't come to much. We erect the awning and eat underneath it, cooler than being inside. We walk Milo along the banks of the Rhône, looking across to the walled town of Avignon. It looks beautiful and we are looking forward to visiting it tomorrow. Milo has his swim, and we have a refreshing shower in the bloc de douche – so hot and sticky – yuk! Milo (just call me mole) sleeps under Escargot. I am tempted to join him, but I know I would be eaten alive by the mozzies which are already attacking me inside the van.

A welcome breeze today and not so humid. Milo has an early river walk and then we leave him in Escargot, which is very shaded so we know he will be cool, and walk across the bridge into Avignon. It is steeped in history with its papal palace and cathedral and the famous *pont* halfway across the

Rhône. We walk up to the Papal Palace but don't pay to go in as it is too expensive. We do go into the cathedral which is typically Roman Catholic and dark and dreary. The gardens and ramparts behind give us a good view of the Rhône.

Wander around the streets and shops. Phillippa is on a mission to find some new shorts. She spots an H&M store, much to her delight. In we go and mission accomplished, she buys some shorts and they are cheap, hooray! It has been good to be able to walk to Avignon today and not have to take Milo. We treat ourselves to lunch at a pavement café. I have the *plat du jour*. It does make a pleasant change to eat out; I only wish we could afford to do it more often. We walk back to our island site. Avignon was lovely, but I have to say it looks more attractive from the exterior than once in the interior.

Very, very windy during the night. Milo actually gets to sleep inside with us as it is so much cooler. Phillippa gets up at 3 am and goes outside to put the awning down as she is worried it may break. I still don't sleep too well as I am worried the trees may crash down and the wind keeps me awake.

We don't get up too early this morning after our restless night. Milo has his last swim in the River Rhône. Do the usual chores and pack up and off site at 12 noon. We are now on our way to Montpellier. Stop off at *supermarché* for supplies. I find a campsite in the Alan Rogers book but it is too expensive... they charge 6€ for a dog!

We carry on to a site at Palavas-les-flots. The heat and humidity have returned. We go straight to the *piscine* and swim. In the evening we walk Milo behind the campsite where there is a canal and he can have a much-needed swim. We sit outside until late. I am being plagued by mosquitoes and have another restless night's sleep. I am being eaten alive and the bites itch like mad.

We spend today on the campsite. It really is too hot to do anything, let alone walk. Milo has many swims in the canal. I am constantly dripping wet with sweat. The only way to keep cool is to swim in the *piscine*. I have given up wearing a bra as it is so uncomfortable and I have to keep washing them, so now I am braless which is quite liberating. Phillippa gets chatted up by two French Algerian lads and they invite her round for a glass or two of wine that evening. They are very gallant and invite me also. I naturally decline. It is good for Phillippa to have some fun. I spend the evening reading, and she returns at 11 pm.

Today we plan to go into Montpellier. We make sure Milo has lots of swims in the canal first and then chain him up to his stake. It is long enough for him to be able to crawl under the van for shade, the coolest place. I leave him a large bowl of water. We catch a bus from outside the site at 11.45 am which takes us to the edge of Montpellier from whence we walk towards the *City Historique* and through a large shopping mall called the Polygone. I find a *pharmacie* and stock up on mozzie spray and cream, along with a smoke ring to burn outside during the evening. The smiling pharmacist bids me farewell with "*Bonne journée, madame*" as I leave. Montpellier is a very modern city and would appear to be beautifully clean and spacious. I read in the "Rough Guide" that it is renowned for its university and has 65,000 students.

We wander down some of the little backstreets, trying to find a modicum of shade as we crawl along beside the walls. I am trying to find a *coiffeuse* as I am desperate to get my hair cut as it is now starting to resemble straw. We enquire at one or two but can't get an appointment until much later. Finally we find one who can cut my hair straight away. The lady hairdresser is really sweet but doesn't speak a word of English. With Phillippa's basic French and a lot of gesticulation, we manage to make her understand what I want done.

The hairdresser hands me some stylist magazines and I point to the style of haircut that I would like. My vision of a chic French haircut proves to be a delusion as I feared, she is somewhat scissor happy and cuts my hair far too short. Still, at least it will last for some time and will feel a lot cooler AND it only cost €10.00.

We walk back through Place de la Comédie to the Esplanade and gasping for a drink, we buy some bottled water and sit in the shade of some trees by a park. We both feel we have not seen as much of Montpellier as we would have wished but are flagging now. It is stiflingly hot. The heat rises from the pavements and there is little shade. We are concerned too about Milo and so return to the tram stop and catch the crowded tram, which has standing room only and smells of garlic breath and sweaty armpits, to the bus terminal, from whence we board our bus back to the campsite. We are relieved to be back, and thankfully Milo is fine. We have to have a nap as the heat has drained our energy. Then it's into the *piscine* to swim and swim. Milo gets to go in the river and then has a much-needed groom.

Dimanche has come around again. The weeks are flying by far too quickly. We do the usual chores; empty water, loo etc. ready to move on. Milo has a final swim in the river and Phillippa and I have a last swim in the *piscine*. We then drive towards Bezier. The countryside is not terribly interesting and I find myself dozing off and then feel really guilty as Phillippa is having to do the driving and I am supposed to be navigating.

Our next campsite is at Villeneuve-lès-Béziers on the Canal du Midi. We love this site as it is really quiet with only 75 pitches and the joy of it is that we are able to walk from the site right on to the canal itself. We partake of our usual swim in the *piscine*, have our supper and then walk Milo along the towpath which is delightful with houseboats moored up alongside beneath avenues of poplar trees. It is much cooler this evening, so we are able give Milo a good long walk for a change.

The following morning we walk into the village of Villeneuve-lès-Béziers which is just over the canal bridge. There is not much in the village, but we do find a local store and buy a few provisions. After lunch and our obligatory swim, we study the map and try and plan the rest of the route. Phillippa blades along the canal towpath and I walk Milo who is almost growing webbed feet as he is swimming so much. In the evening we walk to a little pizza cafe which is right beside the canal. I indulge myself and enjoy a Pastis apéritif, my first since coming to France. We share a pizza and salad and a glass of wine. It is one of the most enjoyable meals we have had together on our trip. We are both very relaxed, we are in a beautiful setting and the whole atmosphere feels very French.

Up and about early and I walk Milo along the towpath before breakfast. It is really peaceful and I enjoy walking beneath the beautiful poplar trees. After breakfast, we saunter into Villeneuve again where there is weekly market, and we purchase some cherries, fruit and olives. We decide not to go into Béziers; we are just enjoying where we are and can't be bothered to move. We plan to go for a bike ride along the canal towpath but Phillippa is unable to blow the tyres up on her bike. So I set out on my own and cycle for an hour and a half and find myself singing along to the words "ridin' along on my pushbike, honey." I feel really happy and uplifted. It is so therapeutic to cycle. There are lots of boats going up and down the canal and I give a wave to people on deck. How wonderful, I think, boating along the Canal du Midi is something I would love to do one day, if only I had someone to do it with. I return to Phillippa feeling very proud of my excursion and tell her all about my adventure. After lunch we swim in the lovely *piscine* which we have all to ourselves which is absolutely fantastic. Phillippa has managed to pump up the tyres on her bike, so she goes for a cycle that evening whilst I walk Milo.

We feel sad to leave this site today where everyone has been so chilled, friendly and relaxed. We shall miss the lovely pool too. Milo gets a really long walk along the canal and he has lots of swims. It is so soothing to be walking under the trees. Escargot is packed and ready to move on once more. We drive through Béziers towards Carcassonne. This was not on our list of places to visit, but people we had chatted to on the du Midi site said we really should visit and the "Rough Guide" said it was a must, so we did. The countryside we travel through now is rather flat and uninteresting. Our new campsite is located just outside Carcassonne which looks spectacular – a medieval walled city with towers and turrets. We can't wait to explore it tomorrow. We are able to walk Milo along a footpath by a stream with Carcassonne in all its splendour in view before us.

After supper, whilst I am at the wash up, I get talking to a Welsh chap who tells me he and his wife have just come back from an eight-week sojourn in Spain and waxes lyrical about how lovely it is there and how much cheaper everything is compared to France. He encourages me to go. I must say it is tempting. There are a lot of Brits on this site; "GB" stickers everywhere. There is a storm brewing and it has become very hot and humid. The wind gets up and we have thunder and lightning. Phillippa goes out at 2.30 am and puts the awning away. It starts to rain, so we call Milo out from under the van and he doesn't take much persuasion to come inside and spend the rest of the night indoors with us. We don't sleep too well as the storm is so noisy and there are frogs in the stream behind which make a dickens of a racket croaking loudly.

By the morning the storm has abated and the air is much fresher and cooler, so we opt to take Milo with us into Carcassonne. Close up, it looks even more amazing, like a Lego castle, almost unreal. We can walk from Escargot along the path by the stream into Carcassonne. I stop to take photos by a bridge and momentarily lose Phillippa and Milo who have gone off in another direction. I wander around for three-quarters of an hour trying to find them and feel quite panicky as I think something terrible has happened to them. I finally find them much to my great relief. Phillippa struggles to understand why I am so upset. "We haven't been gone that long Mum," she says. Now that we are reunited we take a walk around the ramparts and the interior of the old city. It is somewhat commercialised with lots of people milling around and school parties of young children being led by harassed teachers. We find a shaded square with many cafés and enjoy sitting having lunch and people watching. We wander back to Escargot and have a late swim in the *piscine* which is far smaller than the one at our previous site on the Canal du Midi. Later, I get chatting to a Scottish chap who is on the adjoining pitch to ours. He is on his own, but tells me that his wife is flying out tomorrow to join him. They have recently bought a property near to Carcassonne which they intend to live in permanently. When we walk Milo after supper by the stream, he seems full of life and wants his stick thrown over and over again. It must be the cooler temperature which is revitalising him.

Our drive today towards Toulouse and Montauban is most uninteresting being flat, arid and industrial. We are glad to stop for a picnic lunch beside the Canal du Midi where we sit on a jetty in the sunshine and Milo enjoys a swim. We carry on to Cahors and travel through some of the Lot Valley to Sarlat. The countryside is so much lovelier here, green and lush with gentle rolling hills dotted with cattle and hay bales. It reminds me of Devon and home. We are feeling much better now that there is more to see, and we have the windows open as always in the heat. Phillippa is playing some of her CDs as she drives. "My brown eyed girl" comes on and both being brown eyed, we feel it is our signature tune. Turning up the volume, we belt out the song, as I sit with my bare feet up on the dashboard. For a brief interlude I forget I am a fifty-three-year-old widow, and as I sing along with Phillippa, I feel decidedly youthful and happy. We burst out laughing.

We finally arrive at our campsite at 7 pm where we soon head for the *piscine* which is in a glorious setting overlooking hayfields and rocky cliffs above the river. We cobble some food together and then walk Milo down to the river along a sandy beach beneath soaring cliffs which really are beautiful. We meet a couple parked along the river who are camping *sauvage* in their motor home. The husband is French, but his wife is from London originally and they have a collie dog called Teddy. They tell us that they live in Spain but spend a lot of their time travelling. They obviously enjoy a nomadic existence. They have left Spain as it is too hot there at the moment apparently. I can't imagine anywhere being any hotter than it is here in France. We find it very amusing to listen in to their conversation – he speaks little English, but she speaks to him in French calling him "*chérie*" with a very strong cockney accent. Milo and Teddy have a bit of a scrap over a stick but it is all very half-hearted.

It is Saturday morning, and we want to catch the market in Sarlat so leave the site at 10.30 am. We have a job to park once we arrive in Sarlat as it is obviously a popular venue. The market is very long, spreading out along both sides of the street. It is starting to heat up but we take Milo with us. I buy fruit and vegetables including a kilo of new potatoes, some olives and a *demi poulet* for our supper. We treat ourselves to a bag of *frites* for our lunch which makes a pleasant change from a chewy cheese and tomato baguette. Having taken our purchases back to Escargot, we sit and enjoy a welcome cold drink. Leaving Milo in the comparative cool of the van, we walk back into Sarlat to explore. We locate the ancient cathedral and go inside and look around, welcoming the shade it provides from whence, refreshed, we explore the quaint medieval streets with their cream-coloured houses. The sandy-coloured stones here remind me of houses in the Cotswolds. There are lots of British here; it is obviously a very popular tourist centre. Hot and sticky once more, we drive back to our campsite and go for a swim. Afterwards we flake out on the sunbeds and sunbathe. For supper we partake of the demi poulet bought at the market along with a side salad, and then we give Milo a walk by the river. It is a beautiful evening, and the water looks so clear and inviting that other people have taken advantage of this and are swimming in the river. Phillippa decides to join them along with Milo. She tries to persuade me to join her in the water and says it is awesome, but I am not tempted.

Early morning and I am up and out walking Milo by the river. It appears we have now moved into "high season." We had to pay more for our pitch yesterday, Saturday, than Friday when we arrived. It is quite an expensive site anyway so time to move on. We decide to go to another cheaper campsite fairly nearby as we want to explore this region. We drive through pretty countryside and stop at La Roque-Gageac, a well-known one-street hamlet opposite the river with mellow cream-coloured stone houses and an impressive chateau at one end. We want to get out and explore but it is very difficult to find anywhere to park, so we have to carry on to the next campsite. On arrival, we secure what has to be one of our best pitches yet – it is literally right alongside the river. Milo thinks he is in heaven and sits there all day with a stick in his mouth waiting for someone/anyone to throw it for him. He can swim to his heart's content. It is very peaceful here, unlike our last site near Sarlat which was full of children. The *piscine* is fabulous and almost empty. Again, there are lots of British on the site and we become friendly with an English couple and their daughter. By nightfall, the air has become oppressive and humid once more. There is a terrific thunderstorm with thunder and lightning, so Milo sleeps in with us out of the rain.

The air has cleared by morning and the sun breaks through. The advantage of staying on a site for more than one day means I can catch up on the washing. I do a machine load full, and Phillippa rigs up a line so it can be pegged out to dry. We are going to visit Domme today which according to "The Rough Guide" is classified as one of the most beautiful villages in France and occupies a splendid position high above the Dordogne Valley. We find it to be really commercialised, but it does have spectacular views. On our return journey we call at a *supermarché* but find it is closed. Back on our delightful pitch, the English couple next to us very kindly offer to give us a lift to the *supermarché* in their car.

This is great as it means we don't have to move Escargot yet again. It is a real novelty being in a car again after eight weeks.

They are a friendly couple and we so appreciate their kindness. We have our supper sitting by the river Céou. This is definitely Milo's favourite site except he pesters us the whole time to throw his stick into the river so he can swim. The *cigales* are in full throttle here and we hear them constantly chirruping away. There are beautiful dragonflies darting over the river and black butterflies. It is idyllic.

I wake early and love just lying on my sofa bed looking out of the open window. Such a pastoral scene with the early sunlight slanting through the branches of the trees over the river. That has been one of the joys of travelling around in Escargot as every few days I wake up to a different view. I have a pressing need to go to a cashpoint, and so we drive into Gourdon. We are a bit disappointed in the town as we do not find a lot there to see. The old part leading up to the church is quite interesting, but that is about it as far as we are concerned. To be fair, I think we have both overdosed on medieval towns and villages. I locate a cashpoint and try to withdraw money, but it is not working. It has now started to rain, so we decide to head back to our campsite.

We stop off at two more cashpoints en route – one announces it is "shut for lunch" whilst the other one tells me I don't have sufficient funds to withdraw cash, which is somewhat alarming. Phillippa draws some out on her card. I am really worried about the money situation. I sit in Escargot and try and work out how much we have been spending. The trouble is, there is no way of checking my current account. Remember this was in the days before I had internet banking. I cannot believe I am over my overdraft limit. Phillippa and I have a serious discussion and decide we have to "draw our horns in" for the next month and only use the cheapest sites and eat even less. I feel really down about it all. I need to clear my head and so I take Milo for a walk across the fields at the bottom of the site where I meet up with the English couple with their daughter again. The husband tells me he has had two nervous breakdowns and consequently is unable to work. Their daughter I would guess is aged about twenty. They explain that they are hoping to move to a "better life" either here in France or in Spain but are not sure what they will do long term. I tell them about the death of my husband and that is the reason I am travelling with Phillippa. They are full of admiration as to what Phillippa and I are doing and are interested in hearing about the places we have visited thus far.

Although the temperature is now a lot cooler, Phillippa and I decide go for a quick swim in the *piscine*. On walking back to Escargot, we stop and talk to another English couple who introduce themselves as Chris and Dawn. They come from Bristol and it transpires Chris used to work for the BBC. They had very kindly taken our towels and chairs inside when we had been in Gourdon and it had started raining. It is much colder tonight and I need a blanket and bed socks. What a contrast to a few days ago. It rains hard in the night, but it is comforting to hear Milo snoring next to me on his bed under the table. It is a wet, chilly morning, but we feel we should stay another day on this site as we like it here so much. We have a lazy morning and have a lie-in and read our books. Once the rain has cleared, we walk to the hamlet of St. Cybranet and do a small shop at the little store there. My card is still not being accepted, which is all rather worrying, so Phillippa pays on hers. We spend part of the afternoon catching up on emails. Chris, the BBC chap, calls in and invites us around for drinks later. How exciting!

We give Milo a walk by the river first before we join Chris and Dawn where we sit under their awning outside their caravan and enjoy a glass or two of wine. They are an interesting couple to talk to. They let us have a look at their "Camping and Caravan" book and Phillippa copies down the names of campsites on the Atlantic coast where we plan to head on to from here. The sites in this camping book prove to be much cheaper than those in "Alan Rogers." Chris is very interested to hear about the site where we stayed on the Canal du Midi, so we give him the details. The following morning, Chris comes over and helps Phillippa pump up the tyres on her bike which annoyingly keep going down for some reason. He also checks the tyre pressures on Escargot which are really low, so he kindly offers to go with Phillippa to the nearest garage to put air in the tyres. I stay behind with Milo and sit chatting to Dawn. Phillippa returns with Chris to say that the pump is not working at the garage. What a blow this is.

We say our farewells to Chris and Dawn and the other English friends we have made on the site. How transient this way of life is proving to be. We drive to the small town of Monpazier where I find a cashpoint, but once again I am refused cash with a message telling me to contact my bank. I manage to ring my bank on my mobile phone, and the person on the other end tells me I am overdrawn and promises to ring me back but does not do so. I try using a public phone box but discover I have to have a phone card which I do not possess. Phillippa finds a local garage where she is successful in putting air into Escargot's tyres which is something positive at least. I finally get through to the bank again on my mobile phone and speak to a bank employee who can tell me the exact amount I am overdrawn. It is a shock, although it will be reduced since my month's rent has yet to be paid in. I have to increase my overdraft limit which of course I shall have to clear once we return home. We both feel pretty depressed at the situation and cannot understand how we have got into this predicament , we have hardly been extravagant we feel. From now on, we shall have to find much cheaper campsites and not travel so many miles so as to use less petrol. We stop at a *supermarché* and stock up on supplies. I have to pay with my credit card as I have no other choice at the moment. We head on out into the countryside and find a little campsite in a tiny hamlet called Lustrac which only costs 6€ a night. That is much more like it. We have our supper and then give Milo a really good walk into Lustrac where he can swim in the river. Our route back takes us along country lanes, past farms and fields full of crops. We could easily be back in Devon. Very quiet and peaceful. Milo loves being in the countryside again.

After breakfast and Milo's walk, we set to and give Escargot a thorough clean inside. The fact it all looks spruce and tidy makes us feel much better. It is amazing how little one really needs. We feel we have everything here in dear Escargot, our temporary home. There is nothing I miss possession wise, not even television. We finally leave the site at 12.30 pm, and we drive past fields and fields of yellow sunflowers which are so cheery in the sunshine. I find a cheap campsite at 12€ just outside Casteljaloux which is set in a pine forest beside a lake. Unfortunately we are not allowed to walk Milo beside the lake. We meet a Swiss lady who comes across to talk to us with her rescue dog called Caramello.

Our new found friend who is called Sylvia tells us that she lives for six months of the year in Spain, three months in Switzerland and three months in France. How cosmopolitan. We take our bikes down from the bike rack and cycle to a nearby lake and shingle beach. It is a pleasant temperature today so Milo is able to run alongside us. Phillippa has a quick swim in the lake but doesn't stay in for long as it is too cold. The colder water doesn't bother Milo; he is happy to swim whatever. We carry on cycling around the lake through woods and past a golf course. Whilst we are having our supper later on, Sylvia comes over with Caramello to say goodbye as she is off early in the morning. Another parting of the ways; I am sorry to bid her farewell as I really liked her and would have enjoyed getting to know her more.

When we were staying at Col sur Loup way back near Antibes, Dave and Amy the couple we befriended there, had told us about the village of Le Mas-d'Agenais where there is an original Rembrandt painting dated 1611 depicting the crucifixion of Christ. We pinpoint it on the map and drive to Casteljaloux and on to the village of Le Mas-d'Agenais where we locate the church. We have to get a 2€ token from the nearby shop to insert in a slot inside the church which will then "light up" the painting. It really is quite amazing to be standing in a church in a small village in rural France looking at an original Rembrandt. It is an awesome and moving experience and well worth the detour. We are so glad we made the effort to come and see it. From here, we head across country on very straight roads towards Grignols and Saint-Symphorien.-d'Ozon We stop off for a picnic lunch and then I drive for the rest of the way. Phillippa is obviously not very happy about my being at the wheel and does a lot of "back seat" driving which causes a certain amount of angst! I eventually get us safely to Mimizan on the Atlantic coast. We check out a municipal campsite near the beach, but I am not too keen as it looks a bit like a holiday camp and has no *piscine*. I manage to park up near the beach, much to Phillippa's relief, and we walk along duckboards over sand dunes to the beach. This is a real Atlantic coast beach – long and flat with people windsurfing on the breakers. It reminds us very much of Cornwall. We try lying and sunbathing, but it is too windy and sand blows in our faces. We realise that a few people around us are completely naked, especially the men, although it is not a nudist beach! Some French citizens it appears do like to be "*au natural.*" Phillippa is keen to camp *sauvage* for the night along with other camper vans parked nearby. I am not keen as I am in need of a shower and want some proper facilities. We find another site nearby, but it is too expensive. We eventually find one at Camp de Lac. Phillippa is a tad annoyed with me because she wanted to stay near the coast. The site, however, is very pleasant and right beside a lake which we walk Milo around and he has lots of swims.

The early light awakens me, and I lie watching the sun shining through the pine trees on to the lake. I wander over to the shower block for a much-needed shower. There are house martins nesting above which fly in and out, twittering away. I am reminded of the second campsite we stayed on when we first arrived in France which was also by a lake. What a long time ago that seems and has already become a distant memory. Another walk around the lake and then we depart the site and go towards Biscarrosse, which takes us through the Parc Natural Region – pine woods and lakes bordering the sea, crisscrossed with cycle tracks. We stop at a car park (for which we have to pay) alongside the famous La Dune du Pilat which is the highest sand dune in Europe at 117 metres high. We have a picnic lunch and then take Milo with us up the steep steps leading to the top of the dune. We walk along the whole length of it – quite amazing with the Atlantic Ocean on one side and dense pine forests on the other. Walking up and down in the sand feels like being in the Sahara desert. Milo absolutely loves it and digs like crazy, trying to bury his stick and sending sand flying everywhere, much to the great amusement of those around us. We stand watching lots of paragliders going off from the summit.

Reaching the far end of the Dune du Pilat, we walk down the sand from the summit which is great fun. We leave the Dune du Pilat behind and head towards Arcachon which I read in my guide has a municipal campsite close by. We finally find it only to discover that it is not very brilliant and charges 14€ per night, so we decide to keep going in the direction of Bordeaux in the hope of finding something cheaper. We call in at another site but find it is even more expensive. Phillippa keeps driving but we find nothing, by which point it is getting late and so not worth paying for a site. We stay on the autobahn and circle around Bordeaux until we find a service area with picnic tables. It has now gone past 8 pm, and so we vote to stay here for the night. It is free and there is a loo and washbasin in a toilet block. We park on the opposite side from the long-distance lorry drivers. I am slightly apprehensive that we might be accosted by some of the drivers. Once again, I am very grateful we have Milo with us to act as guard. We take Milo around the grassy bits of the picnic area before bedding down for the night after double-checking the door is locked. We survive our first night of camping *sauvage* and I sleep remarkably well as I thought I would be awake half the night listening for "noises." We make use of the loo and basin but miss not being able to shower. We are back on the autobahn by 9.30 am and drive in the direction of Royan. We pick up the coast road and find a beautiful beach at La Palmyre where we park up alongside lots of other camper vans, some of which are huge and have trailers attached towing "Smart" cars. How the other half live! We do feel rather like the poor relations with just our bikes on the bike rack. We walk down to the beach for a recce. It is really quiet and we have a spot more or less to ourselves. The tide is a long way out, so we are not able to swim but we sunbathe and read. On our way back to Escargot, we stop and chat to an Irish mum with her three children who are in a camper van at the camper park.

She tells us they have been coming here for years that it is quite safe and that we are welcome to park up alongside them if we wish. However, we decide to use the designated campsite opposite. We are in need of a shower, and I have to catch up on washing. The *piscine* on this site is very small and busy but we are able to swim and enjoy it. I must say I have missed my swims the last few days.

The following morning we go into La Palmyre and buy a few provisions before returning to the exclusive camper van site at La Palmyre which is right alongside the beach and where we plan to stay for the night. We find our little Irish family and happily park up alongside them. It is fascinating watching all the other camper vans arriving; however, we feel as if we are on a showroom forecourt with thirty plus camper vans surrounding us. Poor Escargot must feel like "Thomas the Tank engine" with large, gleaming streamlined models of modernity towering above him. Never mind, he holds his own. There are lots of children and dogs running around on the site which pleases Milo no end. Some men even have a game of *boules* in the car park.

We get the bikes down from the rack and cycle all along the cycle path to a lighthouse in the distance. Milo runs alongside but gets very puffed. We prop up our bikes and walk down a sandy track over grassy sand dunes onto a fabulous long beach with the Atlantic waves crashing in. We sit and watch the sunset and then cycle back. I have really enjoyed the exercise; it was great fun and exhilarating.

We have survived our second night camping *sauvage* but

in a far nicer place than that of a service station. We are now in "high season," so the campsites can be expensive. It takes us longer to shop around and find cheaper ones. We are told by others that it would not be wise to camp *sauvage* in some areas as there have been a number of break-ins and the "gangs" target foreign number plates. We are quite certain that someone had tried to break into Escargot at one point as we can see how the door has been bent where someone had obviously tried to force the door open. We think that this was probably some time ago when we were parked in a town.

We depart from "camper van city" and drive to the beach which we discovered yesterday near to the lighthouse. We park Escargot by the side of the road and walk down to the beach. We laze away the day reading and sunbathing. Milo has his usual swims and digs his usual sand pits. Phillippa swims but I am content to wade as I am not too keen on the Atlantic breakers. We take a leisurely stroll back to the van where we narrowly miss being fined by the *gendarmes* who are booking cars parked alongside the road. Apparently, vehicles are only allowed to park on one side of the road. One *gendarme* asks us if we are moving on. "*Oui, oui*," we reply in earnest.

We need to find a campsite nearby so as to hook up to electricity and charge up the fridge, have a shower and empty the loo. We return to Saint-Palais-sur-Mer and stop off at a service station to fill up on petrol and get some milk. We find a dear little site at St. Augustine which is very rural and surrounded by fields. It is only 10€ and has a *piscine*. The proprietor is an old French farmer who sits in his shed-like office wearing his cap and slippers. He smells strongly of wine and doesn't speak English. With our few French phrases pertaining to campsites and much gesticulation, we manage to make ourselves understood. We eventually find a suitable pitch and hook up. It is a beautiful evening, so warm, and the sky is tinged with pink. We walk Milo along cornfields past the *piscine*, listening to the crickets which are making a dickens of a racket. We could easily be back in Devon. I have a much-needed shower at 11 pm and feeling very refreshed, fall into bed.

I get up early and walk Milo along the lane by the cornfields again before breakfast. A lovely sunny morning but it is already starting to get hot. I stop to watch two herons flying in and out together as if doing a mating dance. We head for the *piscine* mid-morning, but already the pool is full of jumping, splashing kids. It really is holiday season now. How different to when we started off at the beginning of our trip and would have the *piscines* entirely to ourselves. Those days have long gone. We do manage to swim though and stay in for a long time just relishing the water.

I walk up to the nearby shop and buy *du pain* for lunch. We put the awning up again as it is really hot now just like it was when we were in the Mediterranean region. When it starts to cool off later in the afternoon, Phillippa and I cycle to the local *supermarché* and draw cash out from Phillippa's account. We have left Milo in his usual place under Escargot in the relative cool. We cycle back and go in for yet another swim. After our supper and we have done the washing up, we go for another long cycle ride; we really must be getting fit.

Milo comes with us as we pedal along the flat lanes, past the dykes and cornfields and fields of cattle and sunflowers. It is a perfect summer's evening, and the farmers are out collecting the hay with combine harvesters.

We are up "with the lark" to give Milo a walk and are in the *piscine* before 10 am. This time we have it all to ourselves and swim lots of lengths. Wonderful. We settle up with "Grandad" who is still in his cloth cap and slippers. We drive back to the park de camping sauvage at Palais-sur-Mer and find a space and set up camp. Our Irish family spot us and come over for a chat. Phillippa walks Milo to the beach. I am content to sit under the awning and read. In the cool of the evening, we leave Milo in Escargot and cycle along one of the many designated cycle tracks back towards Palais-sur-Mer. It is another balmy summer's evening, and we cycle along by the sea, passing lots of other cyclists and walkers. We stop at a lovely beach, near to "Club Mediterranean" and have a paddle in the sea. There is a beautiful sunset, and the location would be so romantic if only we had someone to share it with other than each other. What is it about sunsets that make me feel so lonely? When we arrive back at "camper van city" we find that even more camper vans have arrived.

Another early morning start; we take Milo and cycle along to the beach we visited last evening. Milo has a great time swimming in the sea. It is good to be out taking exercise so early before it gets too hot. We say farewell to our Irish family and head off to Mornac-sur- Seudre, supposedly one of France's prettiest villages. It is now 38 degrees centigrade. We manage to park under trees and wander around the village. It is indeed pretty; white- washed cottages with blue shutters and hollyhocks growing all along the streets leading down to a little harbour.

There are the usual arty gift shops. We are glad to go and sit in the twelfth-century church which is beautifully cool. We move on towards Rocquefort but don't stop again as we hope to find a suitable site nearer to La Rochelle. We try various places along the coast, but they are all expensive and crowded. We are getting hotter and hotter and fed up with driving.

Eventually we find a site at Angoulins. It is not particularly cheap, but we have had enough of driving and need to stop. We book in and then walk Milo down to the beach; poor chap, it has not been much of a day for him. The tide is in, so Phillippa goes in for a swim. I go back to the campsite *piscine* but find to my dismay that it is absolutely crowded. The French are on holiday and the campsites are busy by the coast. Teenage boys delight in jumping in, dive bombing and splashing as much as possible. I must be showing my age because I keep moaning to Phillippa that it would never be allowed in English swimming pools where there are rules and regulations! Also we have what I call the "Velcro monkey" couples, what is it with the French and their *l'amour*? The young couples emerge from their tents, head straight for the pool and then cling to each other and kiss each other incessantly in the water. I mean they have had all night! Absolutely hopeless if you want to swim – a choice of horrible dive bombing boys at one end or swooning couples at the other. I am definitely showing my age. Phillippa tells me I should swim in the sea. She is right of course, but I am not too keen on the big breakers.

We are sitting having supper outside Escargot when my phone rings. Our good friends D and C from home are ringing to see how we are. It is so, so good to be able to talk to them. We email, but it is not the same as actually hearing a voice and being able to have a two- way conversation (or three in our case, as Phillippa joins in). We really feel uplifted to hear news from them and to know they are thinking of us.

The *piscine* doesn't open until 10 am but we are there poised and manage to have a reasonable swim before the pool fills up. Today we have planned to go to La Rochelle and are on our way by 11.30 am. Our aim is to find a campsite on the edge of the town. It takes us a while to locate the site I have earmarked and when we do finally find it, we discover it is fully booked. Groan. We drive a little further along the coast to Aytré where there is another site, but this is also booked up. We access a nearby camper van park, but I am not too happy about being there because it is a bit run down and doesn't feel safe somehow. I sit outside under what shade I can find and have my usual lunch of a cheese and tomato baguette. It is swelteringly hot. Phillippa walks to the nearby campsite to buy an ice block for the fridge. She comes back and says that she has been told that there is still one small pitch left on the site. We decide to go for it as we cannot bear the thought of spending a night camping *sauvage* in this heat without access to any water. Decision made, we move on to the campsite. It really is a very small pitch, but it is better than nothing. Once parked up I suddenly realise that I cannot find my wallet and I have a panic attack. I think someone could have taken it when I left Escargot's door open on the car park when I sat outside for my lunch. After a thorough search, Phillippa finds my wallet in a cupboard. I am so distressed I cry with relief. We are both overwrought and worn out with the heat and constantly moving around. Now we have filled up with water I boil the kettle on the gas hob and have a much-needed cup of tea. Peculiar how a hot cup of tea can be so refreshing and reviving in this heat.

We walk across the road to the beach and swim. The sea is calmer today and feels incredibly warm for the Atlantic. Milo swims with us, obviously very relieved to feel cool. Later that evening we give him a good walk along the beach. It is suffocatingly hot in Escargot that night and very difficult to sleep. Milo is back in his "mole" position under the van. There are lots of fireworks going off as tomorrow is "Bastille Day" and a public holiday. Because of the heat we have left Escargot's door open, and Milo, spooked by the fireworks, comes inside panting.

After a restless night I head for the shower block and catch a couple of lads in the ladies' section. I tell them firmly that the *hommes* is next door. I return to tell Phillippa my encounter and tell her to be careful when she goes across herself. We are clearing up after breakfast when these same lads jump over the wall from the road by our pitch and saunter across in front of us and then equally casually saunter back again. They had real attitude and their eyes were everywhere. I used my fiercest voice and said in the only French I knew which was remotely relevant, "Non! Interdit! Non! Interdit! D'ACCORD?" The lads promptly disappeared over the wall from whence they came. Phillippa said, "I think they got the message Mum!" I don't trust these lads at all, and I will be glad to be off this site.

I am relieved when we finally drive away and park on the outskirts of La Rochelle in a car park. From here we catch a bus into the town. It is the first time Milo has been on a bus, but he is very good and sits beside us quietly. We enjoy exploring the harbour and the pretty town and have our lunch sitting on a seat overlooking the harbour. We then catch the bus back to the car park and drive on to a campsite which I have earmarked in the Alan Rogers book. This one is cheap and is in a little market town called Moutiers-les-Mauxfaits. This proves to be a lovely, quiet site, very rural, and so different from the one at La Rochelle. We give Milo a good walk along a marked footpath along country lanes, past fields of cattle and hay bales. Once again, we feel we could be back in Devon. There are more fireworks again tonight, and we sit and watch them from the window in Escargot.

It is hard to comprehend that today is July 15th and we only have one more month left in France before we have to return home. I have very mixed feelings about going back. Some days I look forward to it, but at other times I feel apprehensive about returning and facing the future on my own. As C.S. Lewis wrote "no one ever told me that grief felt so like fear" A part of me does feel homesick as I do miss my home, family and friends. Yet on the other hand I have got used to this "gypsy" way of life and constantly travelling around.

Phillippa and I really like being on this site which is

very peaceful and relaxed. The other campers seem friendly too. They are mostly French. A couple along from us have a large Burmese Mountain dog and they always smile and say "*Bonjour*" as they pass. We can walk Milo along a footpath to the village where we find a quaint little covered market which is set out underneath old crooked beams. We buy some fresh produce. The market has a welcoming atmosphere. There is also a small Spar, so we get a few more provisions from there and carry them back to Escargot. We are definitely brewing for a storm; it is hot, humid and sticky. I do a machine load of washing and then sit outside and catch up on emails. We have a terrific thunderstorm tonight with thunder and lightning. It feels cosy though sitting in Escargot watching the lightning and listening to the heavy rain.

Much cooler today after the storm. We have decided to spend another day and night here and relax. Phillippa hears from her flat mate in London that the girl to whom she sub-let her room is vacating at the end of this month. Not good news as this will affect her and my finances indirectly even more. Still, there is nothing we can do about it at present.

Having recharged our batteries so to speak, we feel ready to move on and drive to Les Sables-d'Olonne, a seaside town on the Atlantic Ocean. We park up on the seafront and have our picnic lunch. There are long, sandy beaches with big breakers and lots of surfers. The beaches on the Atlantic coast remind us very much of Cornwall. We have to stop off at a large *supermarché* and get more provisions. We know that there is a big "Spring Harvest" campsite near Saint-Gilles-

Croix-de-Vie. We have both attended "Spring Harvest" in the past at Minehead in Somerset, and we think it will be fun to go and meet up with lots of other Brits. When we arrive, we are somewhat horrified to find out that to stay there would cost 60€ a night. Dogs aren't allowed anyway so that rules that out. We feel really disappointed and let down. It is obvious that the venue is not really geared up for one-night stopovers and the price does include all the facilities and the visiting speakers. We have no alternative but to drive around and find another site which is cheaper. We do eventually find one alongside a river which is only separated from the sea by sand dunes. Once we have eaten, we walk Milo over the dunes to the fabulous beach. The waves are crashing in on to the shore; they are really big this evening. Phillippa is official stick thrower for Milo who is completely fearless now and charges right into the sea. He goes under the waves and surfs back; he seems to have taken it upon himself to swim for Britain. The sunset is beautiful here… It goes down so quickly the sky changes colour with the sun while the waves keep crashing in. A Dutch guy is so impressed with Milo's swimming he takes a video of him on his camera. I start chatting to him, and being Dutch, of course, his English is excellent. I have wondered many times since if that Dutch man still has the video. I would love to have seen it.

When we finally retire to Escargot, Milo is actually shattered for once and immediately crashes out on his bed under the table which a rare thing. It is a very satisfying feeling to see him in that state as we feel we have achieved something.

We spend virtually the whole of the next day on the beach

and do lots of reading. Milo keeps being a pain and digging huge pits in the sand and sending it flying all over us. He has the whole of the beach for goodness' sake but chooses to dig right next to us and then comes and plonks his wet, sandy body beside us and wants to be "loved."

When we return to the campsite at around 6 pm, we go for a swim in the pool, which we have virtually all to ourselves. Sitting eating outside Escargot later on, we both agree that this is a delightful spot as we look out over the river and the meadows beyond with cows grazing. House martins flit here and there overhead swooping and soaring; it really is a quiet, relaxed and chilled location. We have a little family camped opposite to us; a mum with her two young children.

We wake up to our lovely views over the river and fields. We pack up a rucksack and then cycle with Milo along the cycle track for about 2km into the nearby town of Saint-Gilles- Croix-de-Vie. We leave the bikes in bike racks and have a wander around the harbour, the little antiques market and shops. It is a pretty but somewhat "trippery" seaside town. It is starting to heat up again, and so we cycle back to our site and Milo swims in the river en route. Late in the afternoon, we go and swim in the pool where we are accompanied by the little girl who is camping opposite to us. She takes a real shine to Phillippa and starts chatting away to her in her native French. Poor Phillippa, who until then had thought that her French was reasonably good, is left somewhat deflated, as she only manages to grasp from our little friend that she was called Chloe and that she was five and a half (the half being universally important to children everywhere it seems). Oblivious to the fact that Phillippa has no idea what she is talking about, Chloe carries on chattering and seems content that Phillippa smiles and interjects with the odd "*oui*" and "*comment* ça *va?*" in return.

Today being *Dimanche*, we have decided to drive to the Spring Harvest site in time for the 10.30 am service which is held in a huge marquee. We value being in a church service again and to hear people talking in English. There are people of every age group in the congregation. We sit next to an Irish lady with two children and partake in Communion for the first time in many weeks. At the end of the service, we chat to various people and then wander around the site before having our lunch in Escargot where we have had to leave Milo. We try to decide on the best course of action to take. Phillippa is still keen to stay near the coast and doesn't want to go inland. So we drive further up the coast and try and find a cheap campsite near to the beach. We eventually find one near Notre-Dame-de-Monts which only costs 10€ a night. The site is located in the grounds of a house and the *madame* who owns it seems very pleasant. Having set up camp, we walk across the road through an adjoining field and up over a path through pine trees to the "supposedly" adjacent *plage*. However, it is a bit of a trek and when we get to the beach, we find that it is very busy but having said that, we have to allow for the fact that today is *Dimanche*. We are both starting to regret leaving our previous site by the river which was so lovely, but it did cost 16€ a pitch and *monsieur* would only take cash. This whole situation of trying to juggle money and do the "right" thing is proving hard going.

We spend a second night on this site as although a bit basic, (I had to have a cold shower this morning,) it is cheap. We go to a nearby "SuperU" to do shopping. This proves to be a big mistake as today it is obviously "change over day" and the store is heaving. It is full of Brits like us who are obviously doing a shop for the start of their holidays. We are now into July and the school holidays have begun. All quite entertaining. It feels a lot like being in Tesco on Christmas Eve!!

Decision time. We pack up camp and drive just up the road to Notre-Dame-de-Montes where we find a site opposite designated cycle tracks and just down the road from the beach and it is only 13€ per night. The problem is that the only pitch available has no hook- up facility for electricity. We have decided to stay, however, and just hope that another pitch becomes vacant tomorrow. We walk along the cycle track to a municipal site and buy an ice pack for the fridge which hopefully will tide us over. Once again it is hot and sunny, so we pack up a bag and walk to the beach where we can lie beneath the dunes. I actually go in for a swim as the breakers are not too rough today and the sea is warm. There are lots of youngsters having instruction in sand sailing which is very popular it seems, on these long sandy beaches.

After supper we plan to cycle, but unfortunately the tyres on Phillippa's bike are flat again. She must have a slow puncture. She opts to takes Milo for a walk to the beach, and I cycle along the cycle track to Notre-Dame and go along the seafront. It is a quiet and chilled little resort with lots of holiday apartments which have balconies overlooking the beach. I do enjoy going off on the bike for a change; it is good exercise and relaxing somehow and helps me focus my mind a bit like swimming.

Hooray! The next morning *madame* comes across and tells us a pitch has become available with a hook-up. We move Escargot to pitch twenty-four which is nice and secluded and has hedges on either side. We end up spending two weeks here on the Vendée, the longest time we have stayed in any one place. It is very relaxing not to be constantly on the move and we do love this area along the Atlantic coast and all the cycle routes. I am aware that two weeks is the length of most people's annual holiday and we have been in France for nearly three months.

We are having problems with our emails for some reason. We have been sending loads but can't download any to ourselves. This is very frustrating as we so look forward to hearing from friends and family. It helps to keep us connected.

I discover we have run out of milk, so I set off on my bike and cycle into Notre-Dame to an *intermarché*. I decide to cycle back along the main road as I think it will be more direct than the cycle path. However, I miss the turning to the campsite and go peddling on down the road for ages until I realise I will have to turn back to Notre-Dame and pick up the cycle track and return the same way! I really enjoy the exercise though and feel quite exhilarated. Phillippa is a bit anxious as she wondered why I had been so long. She has had no joy either with downloading any emails. We give Milo a long walk along the beach and over the dunes to Notre-Dame where we mooch around the town. We see that there is a classical concert on in the local église that evening; it is extensively advertised and looks promising, a spot of culture – Vengalis, Bach. We are in dire need of some entertainment and decide we shall go.

An early supper and a walk for Milo is called for and then we walk into Notre-Dame. The concert doesn't start until 9 pm but we arrive early in order to get "good seats" and to buy tickets. It is very warm inside the église. The concert turns out to be an organ recital with one man playing an electric organ with loads of electronic sound effects; loud twittering birds with what sounded like a full orchestra and rushing water thrown in. It was awful. He had electric candles flickering at each end of the organ, but this was no Liberace. In between each piece, our maestro would stand up after the applause and say "*Merci beaucoup*" and proceed to rant on rapidly in French, of which we understood not a word, wipe his brow profusely with a handkerchief and then sit down, whilst we waited for him to fiddle about with all sorts of wires, plugs and gadgets before he proceeded again. I just about recognise "Chariots of Fire" which was decimated. To top it all, we have a fit of the giggles and sit like two naughty schoolgirls biting our fingers until they hurt. We bail during the interval; apparently there is an alto soloist in the second half. The galling thing is that it cost 20€. We could have had a meal out with WINE for that money!! Still, we laugh all the way home to Escargot, so it is probably worth every Euro.

It rains during the night and it is still chucking it down in the morning. Stay in bed and read. Phillippa phones a friend to see if he can advise her how to clear the emails. He gives her some tips on what to try, but all to no avail sadly as it doesn't work. It is still raining hard.

We spend the day reading. Around 3 pm the rain eases off. We are desperate to get out of Escargot and are relieved to be able to walk Milo through the woods to Notre-Dame. We find an Internet café in the hope we can access our emails but no joy. It is so frustrating and disheartening. Walk back in the rain and get really wet. I can't believe it was unbearably hot a few weeks ago. We are just longing for the sun and warmth again and are both feeling down in the dumps.

The sun is out again this morning. Amazing how the sunshine lifts the spirits. Escargot is in a disgusting state, so we spend the morning giving him a good clean. We have a wire brush which we use on the carpet to remove Milo's hair. He has been moulting badly. Phillippa sits outside and grooms Milo which he loves. We all feel so much better now everything is clean and tidy.

Poor old Escargot is looking a bit the worst for wear. He has had a couple of dents and we have lost a few "bits" from him; a wheel hub, the two cones on the top of the roof and the flap over the hook-up. Some of the cupboard doors are hanging off inside. I shall have to replace and repair what is necessary when we return to England in order to sell Escargot. The plan was always to sell him on our return. I know I will not be able to afford to keep him and I will need to recoup some money. However, right now I really don't want to think about parting with our little home.

We drive to the large "SuperU" again to do a big shop and

just as on the previous Monday, it is very busy and full of other Brits who are also stocking up on provisions. One positive thing is that Phillippa is able to pump up her bike tyres (at last) using the air pressure at the garage. Once back on our pitch, we get the bikes down off the rack and cycle towards La Barre-de-Monts along a cycle track. Unfortunately the track is very busy, and Milo keeps getting in the way of the other cyclists and he starts to flag. We head back to camp and wait until the evening to give Milo a good walk on the beach.

I am up early this morning and go down to the beach once more with Milo, so he has a lovely walk. We are then able to leave Milo behind in Escargot with a clear conscience and the two of us cycle all the way to La Barre-de-Monts, 11.8 km each way. It is a great ride through pine forests with different *plages* down to the left. On our return journey, we climb up some wooden steps to a viewpoint at the top looking out across the trees to the sea. We have so enjoyed the exercise even though I am feeling a little saddle sore!

We are really into our cycling now and today cycle in the opposite direction from La Barre- de-Monts to Saint-Jean-de-Monts which is 11 km and continue on the designated cycle path along the seafront. It is a bustling and thriving resort; the beach is packed with people and there lots of cyclists and bladers on the promenade. We both agree that we much prefer Notre-Dame even though it is quieter. By the time we cycle back, I am knackered but pleasantly so. Phillippa walks Milo after our supper. I have had more than enough exercise for one day.

There doesn't appear to be any other Brits on our site. We

have a Dutch couple opposite with their dog and another Dutch family next to us, but everyone else appears to be French. A game of *boules* is an evening occurrence, and we watch the games being played whilst we eat our olives and enjoy a glass of wine.

I am in the habit now of giving Milo an early morning walk along the beach. I enjoy this start to the day and find the peace of walking by the sea helps focus my mind. I am strolling along and see, much to my amazement, that there are a few nudist couples parading in and out of the water. One couple are walking towards me on the edge of the water hand in hand. They are both starkers but unabashed, they greet me with a "*Bonjour madame.*" Keeping my eyes fixed firmly ahead of me, I return the greeting. When I get back to the site, I am somewhat bemused to find Escargot gone and only one chair left on our pitch.

Phillippa appears and explains that madame had come across and told her that our pitch was *réservée* as from tomorrow, so Phillippa had driven Escargot to another bigger pitch at the end of the site. We prefer this pitch as it is much bigger and more in the sun and consequently lighter and warmer. We rig up a line and hang out the washing I had done earlier. Later, we walk along the beach to Notre-Dame. It is market day, and we buy a few provisions and stagger back with rucksacks along the cycle path. It is definitely hotting up again.

In the evening, we drive into St-Jean-de-Monts and park up. Phillippa blades along the seafront whilst I promenade with Milo. There are lots of Brits here and some are enjoying a ride in buggies with a roof on top which five or six people can peddle at the same time.

Quite fun. I am finding it really hard to see all the couples walking along hand in hand, arm in arm. It really brings home to me how much I miss my husband and how terribly alone I feel. How I wish I could be strolling along hand in hand with him! Despite the pain, I feel it has been good to get off the site and do something different.

The days are slipping by all too quickly. We cycle, swim in the sea and lie and read on the beach. Milo gets his walks early morning and in the evenings. We are nearing the end of our two week sojourn on the Vendée. I suggest to Phillippa that we treat ourselves one evening and have a meal out, so we walk with Milo into Notre-Dame and have a meal at the little beachside cafe. I order an Italian salad with Parma ham and mozzarella and Parmesan with a bowl of *frites* to share. We sit outside on the terrace overlooking the sea which is bathed in a glorious sunset. All very romantic if one had someone to be romantic with. I wish Phillippa had a young man alongside her, but at the moment we have each other and for this I am so grateful. Notre-Dame is buzzing tonight with people milling everywhere; it is such a lovely atmosphere – very chilled and relaxed. There is a mini funfair set up nearby and we are content to sit and people-watch.

I have an awful night's sleep. It is so hot and humid – just like when we were back in the South. I get up and put Milo outside so he can sleep under the van as he is too hot inside. This is our last morning on this site; we cannot believe we have been here for two whole weeks. We shall be very sad to leave here but we need to move on and go towards the Loire. I am relieved when morning comes and get up with the sun rise and take Milo down to the beach. I shall miss this walk on the beach each morning, I find it such a positive start to the day. I go back and head for the shower block for a much-needed shower. We breakfast and then start to pack up. A French couple who have been camping near to us come over to bid us *au revoir*. We chat to them for ages and learn that they are called Paul and Evelyn. Evelyn speaks a little English and between that and our basic French phrases we manage to make ourselves understood. They are such a friendly couple, and it turns out they live not far from Annecy. We exchange addresses and Evelyn gives us an open invitation to visit them if we are ever in that region again. We are just sorry that we didn't get to know them better before we were leaving. They kiss us goodbye on both cheeks in the typical French manner. I go to the site office with Phillippa to pay *madame*, who is a very friendly, cheerful soul.

We drive to La Barre-de-Monts and do a shop at a SuperU. The campsites around here are all crowded and expensive, and so we carry on towards Nantes which is in the right direction for the Loire. Escargot is like an oven – oh for air conditioning – we haven't felt like this since Montpellier. We eventually stop at a municipal site in a village called Port-Saint- Père. It is a change to be back on a country site once more. It is a pretty little spot alongside a river with weeping willows. We sit outside under the awning for ages as it is too hot to move. We have our supper, and I give Milo a walk through the village down to the river where he can swim and cool off. Phillippa has gone off on her bike. I think she needs a bit of space from me, understandably.

Up and about early again and we give Milo a quick walk along a track by the fields. The facilities are pretty basic here, but we take advantage of a shower. There is a French family in a camper opposite to us with three children and a kitten, and I am amazed that they all manage to squeeze inside. Many French holidaymakers like to bring their pets with them on holiday, not just dogs and cats but pet rabbits. We were astonished to see on one campsite a couple emerge with their rabbits in a hutch complete with a wire run. Even more surprising was seeing a parrot in a cage being lifted outside to enjoy the sunshine.

We are on the road by 10 am and drive on up through the Loire towards La Flèche. I am back to using good old "Alan Rogers" again and locate the recommended municipal campsite on the edge of La Flèche by a river. There are quite a few Brits on this site. It is the first time we have camped with Brits for weeks. The weather is *très chaud* – hotter than ever. There is very little escape and not enough shade. I lie on the grass under the awning and read. It is just too hot to move. The pool, unfortunately, is heaving with people and we wait, hoping that the pool will empty.

At 7 pm we try the pool again. It is still full of splashing kids, but I do manage to swim; it is so refreshing just to be in water. Later, we walk Milo away from the site into La Flèche which is only a ten-minute walk away. We walk through the centre and discover a lovely park with a river running through it and ducks bobbing along. Milo doesn't quite know what to make of an enclosure which houses miniature goats. We follow the path alongside the river and arrive at the "Hôtel de Ville" which is the town hall and has been cleverly designed to have the river running underneath part of it so that we can walk around it. It is still incredibly hot even at 10.30 pm. Milo sleeps outside. I am woken at 2.40 am to hear two terrifying screams; it sounds as if a woman is being attacked. I go to the open top door of Escargot and look outside, straining my ears and eyes, but I can't see or hear anything. I bring Milo inside. Phillippa in her top bunk is sound asleep and oblivious. It takes me sometime to drop off to sleep again; it has been very unnerving.

The following morning I half expect to look out of the window and see the site crawling with *gendarmes* but all is quiet. Phillippa tells me that she didn't hear any screaming in the night, but I am convinced I did and that I certainly hadn't dreamt it.

I discover that the milk has gone off, so Phillippa cycles into town to buy some more for our breakfast, after which we walk into La Flèche where there is a thriving market and we stock up on fruit and salad items. We make sure Milo gets lots of swims in the river as we walk back. It is sweltering and I wonder why I bothered to have a shower that morning as I am dripping wet already. We are back on the road again by 1 pm and drive towards Le Mans and on to a site a bit further on at Beaumont-sur-Sarthe where we manage to get a pitch right by the river which is fantastic. Phillippa goes to have a shower and realises that I have left the shampoo and conditioner behind this morning – I am definitely losing the plot – the heat is getting to me. Milo spends most of the afternoon swimming in the river, jumping over the dividing fence and having a stick thrown in for him. There is a dear little French couple next to us and they are intrigued by Milo's swimming. The husband speaks a little English and keeps saying, "*Très chaud, très chaud,*" and I reply, "*Oui, très chaud, très chaud,*" fanning my face at the same time.

At 7 pm when it is marginally cooler, we cycle to the nearby public *piscine*, which has been sectioned off into swimming lanes. We get chatting to the supervisor who speaks excellent English. He is fascinated to hear all about our trip and the places we have visited on our travels. He is quite charming. Whilst resting at one end of the pool, having done a few lengths, we also get chatting to a young guy who it transpires was born in St. Petersburg and came to France when he was twenty-two. He speaks English, German and of course French. I tell him I have been to St Petersburg, when it was known as Leningrad, on a school trip. We talk about the conditions in Russia where his parents still live. He works as a translator for the French police. It has been great to be able to chat to some men for a change and have some really interesting conversation.

The swimming was invigorating too and we cycle back feeling on a "high." After supper I go to the wash up, and Phillippa comes across with her phone to say that it is our friend Trish calling from England. It is so good to talk to her. Trish and her husband are the couple with a holiday home in Brittany and who we went to stay with all those months ago. She tells me that they arrive in Brittany tomorrow and plan to drive up to Normandy to meet up with us on Saturday.

I am starting to feel really anxious now about going home; I have got used to this roaming lifestyle. Of course I know we have to return, but the thought of being alone fills me with dread.

A lovely leisurely morning just chilling by the river where Milo sits patiently for someone, anyone, to throw in his stick. This has to be one of the cleanest sites we have stayed on. Phillippa gives my hair a trim. There is an English couple opposite us in a camper van and the wife comes across and asks Phillippa if she is a hairdresser! Her husband joins us and we have a good laugh with them. They are from Yorkshire and normally holiday in Spain where they say it is equally expensive.

Have lunch and pack up and say *au revoir* to our little French neighbours. We are sorry to leave (why on earth did we?). We make a stop en route at SuperU to get petrol and yet more food. Then the nightmare journey begins. Our plan is stop at a site at Falaise in Normandy, but when we get there the site is virtually full. We feel it is too packed and carry on to another site at Thury-Harcourt we are not keen to stay as it is over 16€ a night and not a particularly good location, so we think we will move on a find somewhere cheaper. We end up driving for miles, as they don't seem to "do" campsites in Normandy. We eventually find two sites near Bayeux but they are both full. By now time is going on, and we are both hot and fed up. We drive back to Caen where according to "The Rough Guide" there should be a municipal campsite. We

Expensive campsite right on the beach at 'Camping des Mures' Golf de St Tropez

Morning dip in the Med

Our neighbours washing drying in view of St Tropez

We liked this yacht - its beautiful lines

Plage Notre Dame

Fabulous beach on the island of Ilê de Porquerolles, spend all day swimming in the Med - very hot.

Fabulous pool at campsite above Vaison - la - Romaine, rural Provence.

can't locate it, Phillippa has had enough driving and is getting quite distressed. This is a nightmare. We drive all around the *périphérie* and eventually find signs for the site but to our horror discover it no longer exists. We cannot believe it. Why, oh why did we ever leave Beaumont? We realise it was a huge mistake and were obviously not meant to move.

Eventually by 9 pm we are totally exhausted and have to camp *sauvage* on a housing estate in a small village. We give poor Milo, who has become quite distressed having been shut up in the van all day, a quick walk down a farm track close by. We finally grab a bite to eat and have a much-needed glass of wine before falling into bed.

Wake at 7 am, having slept remarkably well. Give Milo a quick walk in the park opposite and then on the road for 8 am. A really foggy, misty morning. I have found a campsite listed in the "Rough Guide" at Radon on the edge of woods 6 km north of Alençon where we could meet up with our friends travelling from Brittany. Stop off at a small SuperU to get some fresh milk and use the basins in the toilet block to clean our teeth. I am longing for a shower; I feel so disgusting and to top it all my period has started. Phillippa gives Escargot a good hose down in the car wash. She does a good job and gets the worst of the dirt off. Trish phones again and we arrange to meet them in Alençon tomorrow afternoon. Really excited at the thought of seeing them again. We head on for Radon which is a pretty area with lots of way-marked walks through the woods, but can we find the campsite? No way. We end up stopping at a garden centre and I go in and ask for directions. Apparently, the campsite is no longer open! What on earth are we doing? We even debate whether we should go back to Beaumont. We carry on and arrive at Alençon where we locate a tourist information centre. I go in and am told there is a municipal site down by the river. We book in and are so relieved to be back on a designated site once more. Our pitch appears to be opposite a large gathering of gypsies of about seventy caravans. I am desperate to shower and the first thing I do is head for the *douches*. I return feeling much revived. Phillippa thinks we should move to the pitch behind, where it is more secluded, so we do. We both so regret leaving Beaumont which was so cheap and clean and in a delightful spot. We must have had a brainstorm yesterday and have driven miles needlessly and used a tank full of petrol. We were not thinking logically at all. Still we are here now, so no good crying over spilt milk. This site is a bit scruffy and not overly clean. It is unbearably hot again with little relief from it. A camper van with an Italian family parks next to us. They seem very friendly and make a great fuss of Milo, who soon disappears to his old haunt under Escargot to find shade. Then an old French couple in a caravan arrive and park right up close to us. I try to read and doze under the awning. The heat is starting to make me feel quite sick. I am also experiencing pain in my right side which really hurts when I press it. I take some paracetamol. After a late supper when the temperature has cooled a little, we walk Milo along the river where he is very relieved to be able to swim. We walk past the gypsy camp which is quite fascinating; their caravans even have trailers attached which house washing machines. Their dogs are chained up by little kennels. They bark furiously and strain at their chains when we walk by with Milo. We can walk into Alençon which we find to be an attractive town with some medieval buildings and paved streets and squares. It is good to be back in a town again and we enjoy window shopping. It is 10.30 pm by the time we get back to Escargot but still very warm.

A camper van is on the pitch opposite us with an English family in residence. Their youngest daughter, Sasha, who turns out to be nine (going on fifteen!) comes over to play with Milo. She talks for Britain – so self-confident and eloquent. We are given all her family history: dad is a headteacher at a public school and they have been living in Saudi. She has two older sisters. Mother arrives, what a mess! She is certainly the worse for drink and just rattles off telling us all sorts; we can't get a word in edgeways. She appears to be a troubled lady and very affected. What a bizarre episode. We eventually get to bed. Milo sleeps out once more and I leave the top door open to try and get some air inside because it is stifling and humid. I have a restless night, not just because of the heat but also because I still have pain in my side and stomach.

I am relieved it is morning and we can get out into some fresh air and walk Milo again by the river so he can swim. Sasha comes over and reliably informs us that, according to the news, today is going to be hottest so far. I groan inwardly. The family are moving on today; we wave goodbye but it is noticeable that mother doesn't come near us. Perhaps she is embarrassed by her drunken outburst last night. Once I have breakfasted I take some Nurofen to try and kill the pain.

We are amazed to discover that the gypsy encampment has gone. Now there is just an empty field. They must have left in the early hours, all seventy caravans, but we didn't hear a thing. We wonder where they could have gone.

Trish rings to say that they are on their way to Alençon. We arrange to meet them at the Office of Tourism. We give Milo another swim in the river and then walk into Alençon where we meet up with our friends. We sit at a cafe and have much-needed drinks. It is fantastic to be able to. We have a good chat and catch up on all the news from home and are able to update them with ours. We still are not able to receive emails although we can send them. We walk around Alençon and try and find somewhere to eat. Typical there are normally lots of restaurants which always look enticing but all we can find are pizzerias, Eventually, we find a really charming little French restaurant set in a delightful, paved courtyard. We sit outside and Trish very kindly treats us to a delicious three-course meal with wine and coffee to follow. We so enjoy just chilling and chatting to them. All too soon it is time to say our farewells as they have a long drive back to Brittany. We walk back along the river to our campsite. Two more British families are next to us on our pitch now. Yet another disturbed night; it is so hot and airless. We have Milo in with us but keep the top door open. We keep hearing strange noises and at one point Milo really growls and barks at the open door. I get up and look out and see a man cycle on to our pitch and wander around the caravan next door. It is 3 am. This has unnerved me and so I shut the door and all the windows. It is stifling. I can't sleep and keep listening for noises and peer out of the window alongside me. It is really the first time that I have really felt anxious on a site. There is definitely a "dark" atmosphere about this place, and I shall be glad to leave.

I am feeling pretty jaded this morning. I step outside and get chatting to the English "mum" next door. She hadn't heard or seen anything untoward in the night. They are packing up ready to leave on their way back to Cherbourg and then home to Yorkshire with their three children. They have been staying in Cahors, and she tells me that she will be glad to go home and escape the heat which has all been too much. It's not just me then who has been struggling with the temperatures. We too pack up ready to depart. I shall be glad to leave this dirty, scruffy site. We drive on to Le Bec-Hellouin where I have found a lovely, clean, cheap little site in the "Alan Rogers" guide book. Our campsite hosts, *madame* and *monsieur* are quite a double act; *madame* is as round as she is tall and definitely director of operations! We buy some local cider, a melon and grapes from their outlet and an ice cream to cool us down.

The heat is relentless, so humid and airless; it is very debilitating. We try and read underneath the awning but keep falling asleep. We hear the rumbling of thunder and there is a slight shower but it comes to nothing. Rousing ourselves, we walk down through woods which are cool and shaded into Le Bec-Hellouin. A really pretty, charming little village with old Tudor-style cottages and the famous Abbaye Notre-Dame Du Bec which dates back to William the Conqueror. We wander around the grounds and spot a couple of monks in their white habits. We go into the gift shop and admire the beautiful pottery made by the monks. From here we walk more into the surrounding countryside and Milo swims in the beautiful clear water of the leat running through the village. We come across a delightful little restaurant underneath the church spire and shaded by trees. We sit outside on the terrace and order a carafe of rosé and a three-course meal which costs 11€. We so enjoy just relaxing in the cooler air and having a delicious French meal again. We know it will be our last before we return home. We drag ourselves away and walk back up through the woods which are a bit dark and spooky now. It is all uphill, so I am pretty puffed out and sweaty by the time I reach the top.

We take a while to get going this morning but eventually pack up and leave at 11 am. We return to Le Bec-Hellouin and give Milo a little walk in the grounds of the Abbaye and he swims in the leat again. We go back to the Abbaye gift shop and I buy a lovely set of eight coloured plates from the pottery as a present for my stepdaughter. The plates remind me of sweets as they are such gorgeous colours. I also buy a set of three bowls for myself. We drive towards Eu which is above Dieppe on the last stage of our journey to Calais. I have a campsite earmarked but must be losing my navigational skills as I seem to lose the direction signs for it. Phillippa gets a bit irate with me; she is hot and bothered. I suggest swapping places so that she can navigate and I will drive. This doesn't go down too well as she prefers driving. We stop outside a house where we see a dear old chap in his garden to ask directions, which I do by pointing to the name on the map. He obviously doesn't speak any English but indicates that he will take us to the site. He gets in his car and drives down to the town with us following and leads us to the campsite. Dear old chap, it was so kind of him, in this heat too. We proffer our thanks with many "*merci beaucoup*" and smile and wave him goodbye. The site is busy, but we are fortunate and find a pitch under trees. I head for the shower; I need to cool off. Whilst I am gone, Phillippa starts talking to an English family in a large tent next to us. A dad on his own with three teenagers which is unusual. Phillippa tells me later that they are from Birmingham and are staying on this site for two weeks.

The following day, we walk Milo through the grounds of the *chateau* into Eu and have a mooch around. It seems like a pleasant little town. We have to locate a veterinary as Milo will need to be checked over and given a certificate before we can take him back to England. We track down a vets and decide we will return tomorrow with Milo. Back at the site, I am sitting outside reading and get chatting to the "dad" next door. He seems a really lovely man. I think he may be a teacher or lecturer. I tell him all about our travels and where we have been. I tell him that I am a widow. He replies that his wife died last year from cancer and that he is in fact a vicar. It is his daughter's 15th birthday tomorrow and they are leaving very early in the morning to go to Paris for the day. My heart goes out to him and his children – it must be so hard for them. I wish I could have talked more in depth with him about his grief and how he is coping and how it has affected him. We could have shared our experiences of bereavement and maybe have been of support to one another. Sadly, there will not be an opportunity as they will be up and gone before we are surfacing in the morning.

Indeed, by the time I get up the family have already left for Paris. I hope they will be able to enjoy the day despite their sorrow. We walk into Eu and take Milo to the vet (he is not very impressed, poor chap). We are seen by a young lady vet who gives Milo a tablet for tapeworms and treats him for ticks, all for the princely sum of €40.00! But he does get issued with his certificate which means he has a clean bill of health to be able to board the ferry home. We wander back to the site full of mixed feelings. We know that we now have only one more day left in France. Where have those three and a half months gone?

We pack up Escargot for this last time and leave to carry on to Calais. We stop at a campsite near Calais called Autingues-par-Ardres. We cannot believe our eyes when we pull into the entrance as who should be in front of us in their Fiat Swift but Tim and Elouise and their dog Phoebe, who we met all those weeks ago at La Colle-sur-Loup. We couldn't believe our eyes. Amazing. To our delight we end up having the last two pitches next to each other. It really is incredible. We stand and chat and invite them around for a glass of wine later. We give Escargot a good clean and tidy up in readiness for our guests. We give dear Milo a walk around the village and roads. Although we are surrounded by cornfields, there are no footpaths or lanes to walk him on, which is a real pain. We have our last meal together in Escargot, which feels very strange. Tim and Elouise come around, and we sit talking to them for ages over a glass or two of wine. We catch up on where we have been since we last saw them. They spent a whole month on the site in Chamonix walking in the mountains. It appears they are having problems getting the tenants out if their house in England and it means they will have to live in their camper van and camp when they get back. It was so good to talk to them and share our experiences.

We say goodbye to Tim and Elouise in the morning with many hugs. They are leaving to catch the 11 am ferry. We exchange email addresses and Elouise gives me some dry food for Milo for his breakfast which he loves.

We spend the very last night parked on the docks at Calais ready to leave on the early morning ferry to Dover. We are going home after three and a half months in France and having travelled seven and a half thousand miles.

It was very strange once we were back in Dover to be driving on the left hand side once more. Strangely, I remember very little of that return journey home to Devon. I think my mind was in turmoil. Going back to reality and an uncertain future was hard. When we finally turned into the long lane which would lead to my bungalow, I still found it hard to comprehend that our adventure and travels were over. My spirits lifted, however, as we approached my gate and saw a big "Welcome Home" banner spread across the entrance. A friend had lovingly put it there to welcome us home.

Once we stepped inside the front door, another pleasant surprise awaited us. My bungalow was spotlessly clean and shimmering, and on the dining room table was a large bowl of fresh fruit and a big bouquet of flowers. A note lay alongside from two girl friends who had kindly come in and made sure everything was homely and immaculate. My two male tenants had vacated three weeks before and I am sure had done their best to leave the bungalow as they had found it, but there is nothing like a woman's touch.

Obviously initially there was a lot to do, and Escargot had to be emptied of all our belongings. Later we cleaned and valeted him. The lovely farmer at the top of the lane once again allowed me to park the van on his field until I was able to sell it. Another neighbour who was a carpenter did the repairs to the internal doors. I paid him for his services obviously.

I sold Escargot just before the tax was due to expire. I had quite a few prospective buyers who came and inspected him, all of whom were very interested to learn of our trip to France, but in those days most people wanted a diesel van and not a petrol one. I have to say it was with a sense of relief when a couple did agree to buy Escargot. I needed the money and did not want to have to tax him again. Having said all that, when Phillippa and I stood in the road and watched him being driven away by his new owners, we did feel a pang of sadness and nostalgia. Dear Escargot, our home on our backs for three and a half months was gone from our lives forever.

Who knows, maybe the couple who bought a Fiat Swift Royale in 2003 may read this book and recognise Escargot and give him an extra special polish sent with our love. I hope so.

APPENDIX

I did return to work at Paul Property temporarily but was then able to secure a permanent contract at a doctor's surgery as a medical receptionist which I really enjoyed.

I am delighted to be able to report that I have remarried. I met my husband, also a widower, two years after my return from France. We have been very happily married now for fifteen years.

Milo sadly died in tragic circumstances. The sticks which he loved to have thrown for him caused his death. One day out on a walk, Milo dropped his stick at the feet of a stranger, waiting for it to be thrown into a river. The man couldn't resist picking up the stick and throwing it. Milo landed on the stick and it penetrated the roof of his mouth. He died at the vet's overnight on what was my actual birthday. I was heartbroken. The most upsetting thing of all was that I wasn't with him when he needed me most. I felt so guilty and distressed that I had failed him. He had been such a loyal and loving friend. Losing him in that manner took me a long time to get over.

What of Phillippa? She now lives on the edge of Dartmoor and is the proud owner of an ex- thoroughbred racehorse. Riding is her passion, along with her artwork.

I have been fortunate enough to have travelled fairly extensively, before and after my trip to France, to various countries in the world, but my travels around France in Escargot with Phillippa and Milo will always hold very special memories for me.

I will forever be indebted to Phillippa for accompanying me. I could not have done it without her.